edTPA® Special Education

By: LQ Publications

This page is intentionally left blank.

The publication is designed to provide information in regard to the subject matter covered. Information included in this publication are best practices, explanations, and examples. edTPA® is a subjective exam and the publication does not guarantee any results.

Written by LQ Publications

Printed in the United States of America

ISBN- 9781087817224

The author and the publisher make no warranties with respect to the correctness or completeness of the content contain in this publication and specifically disclaim all warranties whatsoever. Advice, strategies, and suggestions described may not be suitable for every case. Providing web addresses or other (information) services in this publication does not mean/imply that the author or publisher endorses information or websites. Neither the author nor publisher shall be liable for damages arising herefrom. Websites may be infected by computer viruses. The author and publisher shall not be held responsible for any damage resulted herefrom. Websites (content) may have altered since the time the author described them in this booklet and this booklet is read. There are no guarantees attached to the publication. The content of this publication is best practices, suggestions, common mistakes, and interpretation, and the author and the publisher are not responsible for any information contained in the publication.

Any services provided by the publication, authors, or company are with the understanding that services can be terminated with or without notice. In rendering services, the author and the publisher are not responsible for any information communicated. Users agree not to hold the service (author/publisher/company) or its employees liable for any services (information) provided or any information displayed on the website. Users release the service from any claims or any kind of damage. The author, publisher, services, and/or company are not responsible for any accuracy or legitimacy of the information provided during rendering services. There are no guarantees attached to services.

No institutions (public or private) have permission to reproduce (in any form) the contents of this publication.

This page is intentionally left blank.

Free Online Email Tutoring Services

All preparation guides purchased directly from LQ Publications includes a free four months email tutoring subscription. Any resale of preparation guides does not qualify for a free email tutoring subscription.

What is Email Tutoring?

Email Tutoring allows buyers to send questions to tutors via email. Buyers can send questions regarding the exam processes, strategies, content questions, or commentary prompts.

LQ Publications reserves the right not to answer questions with or without reason(s).

How to use Email Tutoring?

Buyers need to send an email to lqpublicationgroup@gmail.com requesting email tutoring services. Buyers may be required to confirm the email address used to purchase the preparation guide or additional information prior to using email tutoring. Once email tutoring subscription is confirmed, buyers will be provided an email address to send questions to. The four months period will start the day the subscription is confirmed.

Any misuse of email tutoring services will result in termination of services. LQ Publications reserves the right to terminate email tutoring subscription at anytime with or without notice.

Comments and Suggestions

All comments and suggestions for improvements for the study guide and email tutoring services can be sent to lqpublicationgroup@gmail.com.

This page is intentionally left blank.

Table of Content

Chapter 1 - Introduction to edTPA®

What is edTPA®?

edTPA® is a portfolio assessment developed by the Stanford Center for Assessments, and Learning, and Equity (SCALE) and American Association of Colleges for Teacher Education (AACTE), and the assessment is administered and scored by Pearson Education. Since being used operationally in Fall of 2013, edTPA® is aimed at ensuring the readiness of entry-level teachers on key aspects of education. The assessment allows entry-level teachers to gain exposure to teaching methods and tools prior to entering as certified teachers.

What are the edTPA® subject areas?

The following are edTPA® assessment areas available for students to complete:

- Agricultural Education
- Business Education
- Classical Languages
- Early Childhood
- Educational Technology Specialist
- Elementary Literacy
- Elementary Mathematics
- English as an Additional Language
- Family and Consumer Sciences
- Health Education
- K–12 Performing Arts
- Library Specialist
- Literacy Specialist
- Middle Childhood English-Language Arts
- Middle Childhood History/Social Studies
- Middle Childhood Mathematics
- Middle Childhood Science
- Physical Education
- Secondary English-Language Arts
- Secondary History/Social Studies
- Secondary Mathematics
- Secondary Science
- Special Education
- Technology and Engineering Education
- Visual Arts
- World Language

Overview of edTPA®

The edTPA® focuses on three areas, which include planning, instructing, and assessing. Completing the edTPA® requires candidates to create lesson plans, develop instructional materials, compile students' sample works, develop assessment tools, record instruction, and respond to commentary prompts.

Task 1: Planning for Instruction and Assessment - Candidates are required to develop 3-5 consecutive lesson plans along with develop instructional materials and assessments.

Task 2: Instructing and Engaging Students in Learning – Candidates are required to video record instruction showing a positive environment, instructing students, and engaging students in the learning process.

Task 3: Assessing Student Learning – Candidates compile focus learner's sample work and provide feedback to show progress toward objectives of the lessons.

What is the purpose of the Special Education edTPA®?

The purpose of the Special Education edTPA® is for the candidates to show and to develop understanding in teaching students with learning disabilities. Candidates need to show how theories and research are connected to students' learning along with how instruction is tailored to meet individual needs. The Special Education edTPA® requires candidates to develop an in-depth case study of one focus learner who has multiple learning needs. The candidates are required to identify one learning goal for the focus learner to accomplish in the learning segment. The learning goal must be one of the following:

- aligned with an IEP goal and academic
- aligned with an IEP goal and non-academic
- not aligned with IEP goal but academic

The learning segment must be designed to:

- assist the focus learner to gain knowledge related to the learning goal and demonstrate learning
- reflect IEP identified adaptations of the learning environment, content, and strategies

Chapter 2 - How To Use This Guide?

What is the purpose of this study guide?

The main purpose of this guide is to give candidates an organized and complete presentation on how to complete the Special Education edTPA®. The guide is designed to support students who are attempting the Special Education edTPA® for the first time or students who are retaking the Special Education edTPA®. All information presented in this guide was written for the Special Education edTPA®. In other words, this guide is not a general guide that can be used for any edTPA® subject area. The guide contains clear explanations of requirements, best practices, lessons learned, common mistakes, tips, and examples for the Special Education edTPA®.

How is this guide organized?

The official assessment handbook written by SCALE for Special Education is filled with many pages of excessive information. Students have expressed that the information presented is repetitive, confusing, and unclear. This guide provides a clear, concise, detailed, and complete presentation on how to achieve a passing score on the Special Education edTPA®. The information in the guide is presented in the following sequence:

- The guide starts with explanations of the three tasks for the Special Education edTPA®. Each part of the tasks are discussed in detail along with strategies and tips to achieve a high score.

- A chapter is devoted to explain how to develop Special Education lesson plans related to the edTPA® requirements. Learning goal, objectives, standards, communication skill, and engagement are discussed in detail along with tips to ensure alignment with edTPA® requirements.

- To show students how to develop Special Education lesson plans aligned to edTPA® requirements, the guide includes examples of three learning segments. Learning goal, objectives, education standard, communication skill, and assessments are discussed in each example.

- Learning theories is a critical aspect to the Special Education edTPA®, so this guide includes common learning theories along with examples of how the theories can be applied to Special Education applications.

- Generalization, maintenance, self-directed learning, and planned supports are discussed. In addition, a summary is provided about all the requirements associated with generalization, maintenance, and self-directed learning for the Special Education edTPA®. Examples are also included showing generalization, maintenance, and self-directed learning.

- Three chapters are devoted to explaining how to respond to the commentary prompts. In addition, tips are included on common mistakes and best practices throughout these chapters.

- This guide includes one full example of the Special Education edTPA® portfolio. The example includes lesson plans, instructional materials, assessments, commentary responses, feedbacks, student sample works, and video recording summary. The edTPA® evaluation and scores are included.

How to use the official Special Education edTPA® Handbook?

Candidates need to have the official handbook while reading this guide and developing the edTPA® portfolio as the authors are not allowed to use the exact wording from the assessment handbooks due to copyright laws. Instead of using the exact words from the handbook, in this guide, a reference is made to the prompts or a summary of the prompts are provided.

Reviewing edTPA® Glossary

At the end of the Special Education edTPA® handbook, a glossary section exists. This section provides definitions to some technical terms presented in the edTPA® handbook. Reviewing the terms in the glossary will support the candidates to better understand the edTPA®. Candidates should refer to the glossary in the handbook if they encounter a technical word they are having difficulty understanding.

Chapter 3 - Planning for Instruction and Assessment

Overview of Task 1: Planning for Instruction and Assessment

Task 1 Planning for Instruction and Assessment is to measure candidates' ability to develop lesson plans for instruction along with create meaningful assessments to ensure the focus learner is learning. Candidates are required to use focus learner's interests, strengths, weaknesses, and prior knowledge to develop lesson tasks to engage the focus learner. Moreover, candidates are required to develop assessments that allow the focus learner to demonstrate learning of objectives and standards. This chapter is broken down into five sections, which are required for Task 1 Planning for Instruction and Assessment:

- Part A: Context for Learning Information
- Part B: Lesson Plans for Learning Segment
- Part C: Instructional Material
- Part D: Assessments and/or Data Collection Procedures
- Part E: Planning Commentary

Part A: Context for Learning Information

The goal of the Content for Learning is to provide information about the type of school, location of teaching, and physical facilities. Information about the class that will be instructed is included in the Content for Learning, which includes name of course, length of course, class schedule, and ability grouping.

Some colleges and school districts have their own requirements for teaching, which do not fall within the edTPA® requirements but may impact lesson plans, instructional materials, and/or assessments. These requirements need to be documented to ensure that the graders understand the reasoning behind including these requirements.

Moreover, one of the main purposes of the Special Education edTPA® is for candidates to show the ability to instruct and to assess students with multiple learning disabilities. The candidates need to document detail information about the focus learner's learning disabilities.

The Context of Learning gives the graders background knowledge to understand the approach the candidates took in teaching and assessing the focus student.

Context of Learning Tip 1

> Schools have requirements for candidates to follow in the classrooms; however, only document the requirements that impact the lesson plans used in the edTPA®. Some candidates document requirements that do not impact the lessons used for the edTPA®.

Context of Learning Tip 2

> The requirement for the Special Education edTPA® is to select a focus learner that has multiple learning needs, so the candidates can demonstrate ability to meet the complex needs of a learner. So, when asked to identify learning disabilities, the candidates need to write down more than one learning disability. Failing to do so will result in a negative impact on scores.

Context of Learning Tip 3

> Some candidates think that the Context of Learning is not graded and does not impact the overall score, and they do not put much effort into developing the Context of Learning. The Context of Learning may not be as important as the lesson plans and commentaries, but the document is critical as it provides background knowledge. Filling out the Context of Learning needs to be taken seriously.

Part B: Lesson Plans

edTPA® Special Education require three to five consecutive lesson plans. The Special Education edTPA® require the students to focus on a learning goal aligned with at least one goal in the IEP and, as applicable, relevant academic or nonacademic standards. The instructional setting needs to be unchanged; the candidates need to teach as they normally teach.

The lesson plans are focused on a learning goal, so the plans need to be connected with one another to build on the learning goal. Each successive lesson must include learning obtained by the students in the previous lesson. Taking this approach allows the candidates to see students' progression build toward the learning goal.

Lesson Plan Tip 1

Colleges and schools provide candidates with lesson plan templates, which include many sections. The information mandatory in the lesson plans are the following:

- State Content Standards/Common Core State Standards
- One learning objective
- Instructional strategies and learning tasks
- Communication skills and planned supports
- Generalization, maintenance, and/or self-directed
- Assessments (formal and informal)
- Instructional materials and resources

Lesson Plan Tip 2

Many candidates document a different learning goal for each lesson plan, which is the incorrect approach. Only one learning goal is needed that captures the overarching learning outcome related to the content standard and learning objectives.

Lesson Plan Tip 3

Many candidates writing lesson plans related to special education do not think about expressive/receptive communication skills. These aspects need to be included in the learning activities to make it easier to respond to prompts in the planning commentary.

Lesson Plan Tip 4

Including engaging instructional materials and resources will support the candidate in responding to the commentary prompts. Many candidates do not think about including interactive activities and engaging planned supports when developing the lesson plans. The planning commentary prompts refer to materials and planned supports multiple times, so including videos, visual aids, anchor charts, and engaging supports is a good idea.

Lesson Plan Tip 5

Many candidates document a lot of standards in the lesson plans. They document standards that slightly touch on the activities of the lesson plans, but are not the main focus of the lessons. The key is to include only one standard that is being exposed strongly to the students in the lessons. The selected standard has to be assessed in the learning segment.

Part C: Instructional Materials

edTPA® requires candidates to submit instructional materials related to the each lesson plan. Both originally developed materials and/or third party materials are required to be included in this section. edTPA® only allows candidates to submit 5 pages of instructional materials for each lesson plan, so key critical materials need to be included.

Instructional Material Tip 1

> When using PowerPoint slides, the best approach is to use six slides per page as oppose to one slide per page. Or, only include slides that are critical to the objective of the lesson.

Instructional Material Tip 2

> Don't confuse assessment documents for instructional materials. Worksheets that students independently complete during instruction are considered assessments. Rubrics used during instruction to assess are not included in the instructional materials document.

Instructional Material Tip 3

> Pictures can be taken of equipments, objects, and resources. For example, if the lesson plan includes computers, then taking a picture of a computer and including it in the instructional materials is acceptable.

Instructional Material Tip 4

> Pictures of whiteboard, chalkboard, and Smart Board are acceptable to include in the instructional materials document.

Instructional Material Tip 5

> Materials that are selected in the learning segment have to target the needs of the focus learner. For example, if the student has information processing disorder, perhaps included anchor charts is a good idea. If the student is a visual learner, then perhaps videos can be included.

Instructional Material Tip 6

> The instructional materials need to be organized in order of how there are introduced in the learning segment. All instructional materials need to have the lesson plan number labeled.

Part D: Assessments

Assessments are a critical aspect to ensure the focus learner is progressing toward achieving the learning goal, objectives, and educational standard. Assessments are done prior to instruction, during instruction, and after instruction. For the Special Education edTPA®, assessments need to include blank copies of all written assessments and/or data sheets, including data collection procedures for any oral or performance assessments. Daily assessment records need to be included to monitor the focus learner's progress toward all lesson objectives.

Assessment Tip 1

> To obtain a high score, include both formal and informal assessments that are aligned with the learning goal and measures students' competencies on the objectives and standards.

Assessment Tip 2

> For Special Education edTPA®, worksheets are not always going to be ideal. Candidates can have students perform activities (oral assessments) during class, so candidates need to document the instructions given to the students along with rubric or rating scale.

Assessment Tip 3

> One of the commentary prompts focuses on explaining how candidates involve focus learner in monitoring his/her own learning progress. So, when developing assessments, keep in mind that the focus learner has to be involved in self-monitoring learning.

Assessment Tip 4

> Design assessments where feedback is provided to the focus learner and have activities for the focus learner to use that feedback within the learning segment. One of the commentary prompts focuses on explaining how the focus learner is able to use feedback given to them. By keeping this in mind while developing the assessments, responding to the commentary prompt will be easier.

Assessment Tip 5

> Baseline data is required in the Special Education edTPA®. Baseline data is pre-instructional level of knowledge and/or skill, and the information from the baseline data is used later for comparison purposes. Typically, candidates develop an assessment for baseline data similar to the questions that will be asked in assessments in the learning segment. Taking this approach makes comparing focus learner's learning much easier. Other ways to collect baseline data are curriculum-based measure, work sample, skills checklist, observational notes, or a skills test.

Assessment Tip 6

> When developing assessments for Task 1, candidates should keep in mind the requirements for Task 3, which focuses solely on assessing student learning. The documents to submit for Special Education edTPA® Task 3 – Assessing Student Learning are the following:
>
> - Focus Student Work Sample
> - Completed Daily Assessment Records and Baseline Data
> - Evidence of Feedback

Assessment Tip 7

> The assessments need to be organized in order of how there are introduced in the learning segment. All assessments need to have the lesson plan number labeled.

Assessment Tip 8

> The baseline assessment is not included in Task 1 Part D. The baseline assessment information is included in Task 3 Part B.

Part E: Planning Commentary

The planning commentary consists of a series of prompts related to the learning goal, knowledge of focus student, supporting focus learner in learning, supporting learning through communication, and monitoring learning. edTPA® graders look at many students' edTPA®, so candidates need to clearly and directly respond to commentary prompts.

Planning Commentary Tip 1

> Candidates should read the planning commentary prompts prior to developing lesson plans and assessments, so they know the expectations. Responding to the commentary prompts will be much easier if the elements are included in the lesson plans and assessments.

Planning Commentary Tip 2

Some candidates write the planning commentary after doing the video(s). Candidates need to make sure the responses to the planning commentary prompts are in the future tense.

Planning Commentary Tip 3

Incorporating theories and research into planning commentary prompts can be boring and time consuming. When indicated to include research and theories, candidates need to provide detail information.

Planning Commentary Tip 4

For the commentary responses, the requirement is to use Arial font with size of 11 point type. The document needs to be single space with 1" margins on all sides. Graders can refuse to score the edTPA® if the font, size, and margin requirements are not satisfied.

This page is intentionally left blank.

Chapter 4 - Instructing and Engaging Students

Task 2 Instructing and Engaging Students in Learning requires candidates to submit video clip(s) of teaching the focus student. edTPA® graders are looking to see if candidates are able to support and engage the focus student, deepen focus learner's learning, use instructional strategies and planned supports, and provide feedback. The goal of the task is to see how candidates promote positive learning environment, engage focus learner in learning, and strengthen focus learner's competencies. Task 2 Instructing and Engaging Students in Learning includes two parts, which include:

- Part A: Video Recording
- Part B: Instructional Commentary

Part A: Video Recording

Special Education edTPA® requires one or two video clip(s) (totaling no more than 20 minutes, but not less than 3 minutes). With the limit on the minutes that can be submitted for the video(s), candidates are not going to be able to show everything. To maximize points, the video(s) should include the following:

- providing a positive learning environment
- showing respect for and rapport for all learners
- instructing focus learner on the learning goal
- engaging and motivating focus learner in learning
- monitoring focus learner's learning during learning task(s)
- connecting learning to prior knowledge, personal asset, cultural asset, and community asset
- facilitating the development or application of a self-directed learning strategy for the learning goal
- providing opportunities to apply feedback

Video Recording Tip 1

> Make sure that students are heard loud and clear in the video(s). During video recording, students who talk with a low voice instruct them to repeat themselves louder. Or, candidates can repeat the students' responses and questions. Taking this approach will prevent candidates from having to include a transcript of the video clip(s).

Video Recording Tip 2

When the focus learner gets a question incorrect, don't jump to correct them. Provide feedback that can support him/her to attain the correct answer and allow him/her to make another attempt. If the student is still incorrect, the candidate can provide the correct answer. edTPA® graders want to see how candidates provide feedback and how the focus learner used the feedback provided.

Video Recording Tip 3

When instructing, the candidates need to consider self-directed learning strategies and self-determination in learning. Many candidates do not take this into consideration; subsequently, responding to commentary prompts becomes challenging.

Video Recording Tip 4

Video(s) have to be continuous and unedited with no interruptions. The candidates can only crop video(s).

Video Recording Tip 5

When video recording, make sure to position the camera so that the students' faces can be seen as oppose to the back of their heads.

Video Recording Tip 6

Make sure to capture the focus learner using communication skill along with any supports related to the communication skill.

Part B: Instruction Commentary

The purpose of the instruction commentary is for candidates to provide details and to analyze instruction to demonstrate a positive environment, engagement, and competency development. Responses to the commentary prompts need to be concise and clear without any unnecessary information. Graders like to see example references from the video(s) when responding to commentary prompts.

Instruction Commentary Tip 1

Read the instruction commentary prompts prior to video recording. Knowing what prompts are in the commentary will help the candidates to know what to do when teaching. This will make responding to these prompts much easier. Some of the prompts related to the instruction commentary include:

- how the candidates demonstrated mutual respect, rapport, and responsiveness
- how the candidates challenged and engaged the focus learner
- how instruction was linked to focus learner's prior learning and personal, family, cultural, and/or community assets
- how strategies were used to move the focus learner toward independently initiate and/or maintain engagement in learning tasks

Instruction Commentary Tip 2

Provide as many examples as possible from the video(s). Some candidates just write without referencing the video(s). The entire purpose of the commentary is to discuss the video(s). Every example used has to be referenced. Try not to include examples that are not in the video(s).

Instruction Commentary Tip 3

Using the same reference from the video(s) multiple times is acceptable. Some candidates think that they have used the example and time reference in one prompt that there are not allowed to use the same example again. This thinking is incorrect.

Instruction Commentary Tip 4

For the commentary responses, the requirement is to use Arial font with size of 11 point type. The document needs to be single space with 1" margins on all sides. Graders can refuse to score the edTPA® if the font, size, and margin requirements are not satisfied.

This page is intentionally left blank.

Chapter 5 - Assessment Students' Learning

Special Education edTPA® Task 3 is focused on gathering evidence of the focus learner's learning, providing meaningful feedback, planning future instruction, and showing use of communication skill(s) to develop content understanding. The graders are looking for assessments and feedback that show the focus learner developing competencies in the lesson objectives for the learning goal.

For Task 3, the candidates are to submit baseline data, daily assessment records, and work sample. The selected evidence need to be strongly related to the objectives and standards of the lessons and give students ample opportunities to show learning. For the Special Education edTPA®, the baseline data has to be related to the learning goal, and the daily assessment records have to capture learning related to the objectives.

Task 3 Assessing Students' Learning is broken down in the following parts:

- Part A: Work Sample
- Part B: Completed Daily Assessment Records and Baseline Data
- Part C: Evidence of Feedback
- Part D: Assessment Commentary

Part A: Work Sample

edTPA® requires candidates to submit one work sample that strongly demonstrates the learning acquired by the focus student. The work sample selected has to be completed by the focus learner alone, not a product developed as part of a group. The selected sample can be a test, performance assessment, or assignment from the learning segment. Work sample selected can be one of the following:

- worksheet (test, completed class assignment)
- a timestamp reference from video (no more than 2 minutes) submitted for Task 2
- an additional video clip (no more than 2 minutes)

Student Work Samples Tip 1

> Select an assessment that is meaningful and target the objective of the lesson. In other words, don't include worksheet with only two questions for the students to answer. Have assessment where the focus learner is completing multiple activities or questions that give him/her multiple opportunities to demonstrate learning.

Student Work Samples Tip 2

> Any worksheet included should only have the handwriting of the focus student. Candidates should not provide feedback on student sample work for Task 3 Part A – Work Sample.

Student Work Samples Tip 3

> Making additional backup copies of the focus learner's sample work is not a bad idea in case mistakes are made when writing feedback.

Student Work Samples Tip 4

> Some candidates include all the assessments of the learning segment that the focus learner completed, which is an incorrect approach. No mandatory requirement exists to include all the assessments.

Part B: Completed Daily Assessment Records and Baseline Data

Baseline data is information acquired prior to instruction and often used to compare with data acquired after instruction. Baseline data can be obtained in many different ways, such as systematic observations, teacher-made tests, curriculum-based measures, IEP, or prior instructional history. Baseline data has to capture information about knowledge the focus learner has related to the objectives and learning goal of the learning segment.

For each lesson, the candidates need to have a daily assessment record for the focus learner that captures student's learning related to the lesson. The key for the daily assessment record is to document student's learning related to the objective, and below are few examples of daily assessment records.

Completed Daily Assessment Records and Baseline Data Tip 1

> Daily assessment records are not necessary the worksheets or assignments that the focus learner completed. Daily assessment records should capture overall learning during the lesson.

Completed Daily Assessment Records and Baseline Data Tip 2

> Baseline data is information that is acquired prior to starting the learning segment. In addition, do not have pre-assessments in each lesson plan. In addition, do not have a step in the lesson plan indicating that the focus learner will complete the baseline assessment.

Example 1

Daily Assessment Record

Objective/Lesson	Learning Tasks (without prompts)	Learning Tasks (with prompts)	Accuracy (without prompts)	Accuracy (without prompts)
Lesson 1	Summary:	Summary:		
Lesson 2	Summary:	Summary:		
Lesson 3	Summary:	Summary:		
Lesson 4	Summary:	Summary:		
Lesson 5	Summary:	Summary:		

Example 2

Daily Assessment Records

LESSON NUMBER:

QUESTION 1

Did the student participate when called upon?

QUESTION 2

Did the student participate in paired activity and/or group activity?

QUESTION 3

Did the student provide correct responses when called upon?

QUESTION 4

Did the student show learning toward the objective of the lesson?

QUESTION 5

What score did the student receive on worksheet? Document student's performance related to the worksheet.

Part C: Evidence of Feedback

For the assessment selected for analysis, candidates are required to provide feedback. Feedback can be provided either with video/audio and/or on sample works. Feedback provided to the focus learner can't be general feedback. The feedback has to be detailed and directly related to the student's performance. Explain what the student did correct and incorrect along with how the student can improve.

Evidence of Feedback Tip 1

Make sure to always correct the student's work when questions are incorrect. Just don't mark it wrong without providing some feedback.

Evidence of Feedback Tip 2

Graders look for feedback when focus learner is incorrect and how candidates addressed incorrect responses/answers. However, graders also look at positive feedback provided by the candidates. Make sure to provide both positive and improvement feedback.

Evidence of Feedback Tip 3

Don't give the focus learner general feedback; feedback has to be detailed related to the focus learner's strength and weaknesses. The graders will immediately spot general feedback, which will result in losing points.

Evidence of Feedback Tip 4

Candidates should circle, highlight, or underline any mistakes on the worksheet and make sure the final grade is circled on the top of the paper. Also, candidates can use a red pen to grade and to provide feedback.

Part D: Assessment Commentary

The assessment commentary is focused on analyzing focus learner's learning, providing feedback to foster learning, using language to further learning, and planning future activities. For the Special Education edTPA®, the commentary prompts are going to focus on ensuring the focus learner was progressing to achieve the learning goal.

Assessment Commentary Tip 1

Candidates should read the assessment commentary prompts prior to going to the assessment phase, so they know the expectations. Responding to the commentary prompts will be much easier if the elements are included in the lesson plans and assessments.

Assessment Commentary Tip 2

When providing analysis of focus learner's performance, reference the baseline data, assessments, and daily assessment records as much as possible to support the analysis.

Assessment Commentary Tip 3

When responding to commentary prompts, discuss both qualitative and quantitative data to increase chances of getting a higher score.

Instruction Commentary Tip 4

For the commentary responses, the requirement is to use Arial font with size of 11 point type. The document needs to be single space with 1" margins on all sides. Graders can refuse to score the edTPA® if the font, size, and margin requirements are not satisfied.

Chapter 6 - Developing edTPA® Lesson Plans

One of the first documents that is required by the candidates to develop is the lesson plans. The lesson plans establish the core foundation of the edTPA®, so developing lesson plans compliant to edTPA® requirements is critical. Moreover, lesson plans need to be designed to where other teachers can instruct steps without having difficulty following the plans. This section provides information to develop lesson plans that are aligned with the edTPA®. The chapter contains the following sections:

- Learning Goal, Objectives, and Standards
- Communication Skills
- Activities and Instruction to Engage Students
- Lesson Plan Outline

Learning Goal, Objectives and Standards

Learning Goal

The learning goal is a short-term learner outcome of the learning segment, which consist of 3 to 5 lessons. Special Education edTPA® requirements for the learning goal must fulfill one of the following:

- aligned with an IEP goal and academic
- aligned with an IEP goal and non-academic
- not aligned with IEP goal but academic

Learning Goal – Tip 1

Many candidates write one learning goal for each lesson plan, which is incorrect. The learning goal is just 1-2 sentences, which provides overarching information on the skill(s) for the learning segment.

Learning Goal – Tip 2

- When brainstorming the learning goal, the candidates need to think about planned supports that can be used to support the focus learner in achieving the learning goal. Planned supports include learning environment, instructional strategies, learning tasks, materials, accommodations, assistive technology, prompts, and modifications.

Learning Goal – Tip 3

All lesson plans in the learning segment have to be linked back to achieving the learning goal.

Objectives

Special Education edTPA® requirements for the objectives are the following:

- measurable learning outcome
- enable focus learner to achieve the learning goal

Objective – Tip 1

> The objectives written have to clearly address how the focus learner will master the requirements of the selected standard.

Objective – Tip 2

> The objectives can't be general or vague; the objectives have to be detailed. One approach to take is to include a verb describing what the student will need to do, what the student will use to accomplish the goal, and vocabulary of the standard(s). The key is for the objective to be measurable.

Objective – Tip 3

> When developing objectives, keep in mind the multiple learning disabilities the focus learner has and ensure those are taken into account for the focus learner to achieve the objectives.

Objective – Tip 4

> Special Education edTPA® only requires one objective per lesson plan. Many candidates are used to including multiple objectives, which is unnecessary.

Educational Standards

Special Education edTPA® requirements for selecting a standard are the following:

- standard come from state-adopted content standards and/or Common Core State Standards
- standard selected must be linked to the objectives and learning goal
- standard selected must be assessed during the learning segment

Standards – Tip 1

> Candidates need to include the number and text of the standard that is going to be addressed. If only a segment of a standard is being used, then only list that part or parts that are related to the lesson plan.

Standards – Tip 2

> The requirement for Special Education edTPA® is to only include one standard related to the learning goal. Even if multiple standards are addressed in the learning segment, candidates need to only document one standard.

When developing learning goal, objectives, and learning tasks, candidates need to keep instruction grade appropriate to ensure that all students are able to acquire the knowledge related to the lessons. The lesson plans need to be connected to one another and each successive lesson plan needs to build on the previous lesson to ultimately achieve the learning goal. The following are suggested steps to take to develop ideas:

1. write the learning goal for the learning segment
2. find the academic standard that is linked to the learning goal
3. write one objective for each lesson plan
4. jot down activities that will be completed in each lesson plan
5. revisit the learning goal and make sure it connects to the objectives, learning tasks, and standard

Communication Skills

For the Special Education edTPA®, communication skill is ways that communication is used by the students to engage in the learning tasks and/or show their learning. The skill can target on understanding or interpreting communication or the actual use of the skill. Associated communication supports are strategies and prompts used to support students in learning or using the communication skill. Two key terms related to communication skill are receptive language and expressive language.

Receptive Language – the ability to understand and comprehend what is being said or read

Expressive Language – the ability to communicate with others using language

Activities and Instruction to Engage Students

Special Education edTPA® requires candidates to include activities that actively engage focus learner in the learning. Opportunities need to exist in the lesson plans that allow the focus learner to interact, engage, and practice related to the objective of the lesson. Many approaches can be taken to engage and to interact the focus student, some include:

- establish relationships and connections with students
- show passion for the subject area
- require students to read
- making learning real
- hands-on activities
- integrate students' interests in activities
- recognize students' efforts
- incorporate technology into the lessons
- check understanding throughout the learning segment
- include group and paired activities
- guiding students to reach correct answers or proper skills
- show demonstrates of skills
- direct instruction
- guided discovery
- problem solving
- tactical approach

Lesson Plan Outline

Many lesson plan templates exist, and some candidates get confused what to include in the lesson plans. Moreover, some colleges and universities force candidates to use a certain template. There is no one template that is the correct template. However, candidates need to include only relevant sections in the lesson plan. The following is a suggested outline to use for each lesson plan:

- Lesson Title
- Grade Level
- Learning Goal
- Objective
- Educational Standard
- Instructional Materials/Resources
- Instructional Procedures (detail steps to instruction)
- Instructional Strategies (what instructional strategies will be used in the lesson)
- Communication Skill and Planned Supports
- Generalization, Maintenance, and/or Self-Directed Use of Knowledge and Skills
- Assessments (Formal and Informal)

Lesson Plan Tip 1

Avoid including too many unnecessary details in the lesson plans. Instructional procedure section needs to be the most detailed section of the lesson plans.

Lesson Plan Tip 2

Many colleges and universities give templates to candidates that include sections that are addressed in the planning commentary. Avoid addressing prompts from planning commentary in the lesson plans.

Lesson Plan Tip 3

Avoid using templates that have pre-populated prompts as it takes up space. In addition, avoid using templates with tables. Best approach is to use an outline.

This page is intentionally left blank.

Chapter 7 - Brainstorming Ideas – Getting Started

Special Education edTPA® can be a taunting task to start with all the new terminology, documentations, requirements, information, and expectations. Most candidates have never been exposed to edTPA® and struggle to start the process. Many colleges and universities do not even provide detail support to guide candidates in the right direction to start the edTPA®.

One of the first key documents, perhaps even the most critical document, is the lesson plans. The lesson plans set the foundation for the edTPA®. To have a strong edTPA®, candidates need to brainstorm ideas and learning activities that will connect the learning goal, objectives, standard, and communication skill to support focus learner in acquiring knowledge.

This chapter will cover several brainstorming of lesson plans for the following:

- First Grade – Compare and Contrast Informational Text
- First Grade – Adding Within 20s
- Third Grade – Parts of Speech

First Grade – Compare and Contrast Informational Text

Learning Goal

The learning goal is for the focus learner to compare and contrast informational text by acquiring knowledge of vocabulary, participating in in-class activity, and answering comprehension questions.

Grade Level

First Grade

Lesson 1

Objective

> The objective for the lesson is to articulate, understand, and use vocabulary words, included in the informational text, by completing a worksheet related to the vocabulary words.

Educational Standard

> CCSS.ELA-Literacy.RI.K.1 - With prompting and support, ask and answer questions about key details in a text.

Communication Skill

> The communication skill required in this lesson is answering questions.

Informal Assessment

> After teaching the vocabulary words, the teacher will ask the students check for understanding questions by asking to use vocabulary words in sentences.

Formal Assessment

> The students will be required to complete a worksheet related to the vocabulary words introduced in the lesson.

Lesson 2

Objective

The objective is for the focus learner to read text (Jack the Runner) with minimal support and answer check for understanding questions related to details in the text.

Educational Standard

CCSS.ELA-Literacy.RI.K.1 - With prompting and support, ask and answer questions about key details in a text.

Communication Skill

The communication skill required in this lesson is answering questions.

Informal Assessment

The students will work in pairs to read an information text along with answer comprehension questions.

Formal Assessment

The students will be required to complete a worksheet with open ended questions and multiple choice questions related to main idea, characters, and events in the passage.

Lesson 3

Objective

The objective for the lesson is to read text (Helping Hands) with minimal support and answer check for understanding questions related to details in the text.

Educational Standard

CCSS.ELA-Literacy.RI.K.1 - With prompting and support, ask and answer questions about key details in a text.

Communication Skill

The communication skill required in this lesson is answering questions.

Informal Assessment

The students will work in pairs to read an information text along with answer comprehension questions.

Formal Assessment

The students will be required to complete a worksheet with open ended questions and multiple choice questions related to main idea, characters, and events in passage.

Lesson 4

Objective

The objective for the lesson is to complete a Venn Diagram related to the text Jack the Runner and Helping Hands.

Educational Standard

CCSS.ELA-Literacy.RI.K.1 - With prompting and support, ask and answer questions about key details in a text.

Communication Skill

The communication skill required in this lesson is answering questions.

Informal Assessment

The students will work in pairs to re-read Jack the Runner and Helping Hands. While the students are reading, I will be observing students.

Formal Assessment

The students will be required to complete a Venn Diagram related to the text Jack the Runner and Helping Hands.

First Grade – Adding Within 20s

Learning Goal

The focus learner will gain knowledge in adding and subtracting within 20 to be able to solve word problems involving addition and subtraction within 20.

Grade Level

First Grade

Lesson 1

Objective

> The objective of the lesson is for the students to gain knowledge of adding within 20 by completing a worksheet.

Educational Standard

> CCSS.Math.Content.1.OA.C.6 - Add and subtract within 20, demonstrating fluency for addition and subtraction within 10.

Communication Skill

> The communication skill related is answering questions through the principal of counting. The students will be required to answer questions during instruction and when completing assessment.

Informal Assessment

> The teacher will observe the students when using blocks, fingers, and tallies in adding within 20 during in class activity.

Formal Assessment

> The students will complete a worksheet involving adding within 20 related to the methods introduced in the lesson.

Lesson 2

Objective

The objective of the lesson is for the students to gain knowledge of subtracting within 20 by completing a worksheet.

Educational Standard

CCSS.Math.Content.1.OA.C.6 - Add and subtract within 20, demonstrating fluency for addition and subtraction within 10.

Communication Skill

The communication skill related to the lesson is answering questions through the principal of counting. The students will be required to answer questions during instruction and when completing assessment.

Informal Assessment

The teacher will observe the students when using blocks, and tallies to see if the students understand the information being presented to them.

Formal Assessment

The students will complete a worksheet involving subtracting within 20 related to the methods introduced in the lesson.

Lesson 3

Objective

The objective of the lesson is to acquire knowledge of adding and subtracting together within 20 by completing a worksheet.

Educational Standard

CCSS.Math.Content.1.OA.C.6 - Add and subtract within 20, demonstrating fluency for addition and subtraction within 10.

Communication Skill

The communication skill related to the lesson is answering questions through the principal of counting. The students will be required to answer questions during instruction and when completing assessment.

Informal Assessment

The students will be observed as they explain how to solve the problems to their peers.

Formal Assessment

The students will complete a worksheet related to adding and subtracting together within 20.

Lesson 4

Objective

The objective of the lesson is to solve basic word problems involving addition, subtraction, or addition and subtraction together within 20.

Educational Standard

CCSS.Math.Content.1.OA.C.6 - Add and subtract within 20, demonstrating fluency for addition and subtraction within 10.

Communication Skill

The communication skill related to the lesson is answering questions through the principal of counting. The students will be required to answer questions during instruction and when completing assessment.

Informal Assessment

The students will be observed when using blocks and tallies to see if they understand the information presented to them.

Formal Assessment

The students will complete a worksheet related to solving basic word problems involving addition, subtraction, or addition and subtraction together within 20.

Third Grade – Parts of Speech

Learning Goal

The focus learner will understand, recognize, and use nouns, pronouns, verbs, adjectives, and adverbs when reading and writing.

Grade Level

Third Grade

Lesson 1

Objective

> The objectives of the lesson are to understand the function of nouns and pronouns, identify nouns and pronouns, and write sentences using nouns and pronouns.

Educational Standard

> Literacy.L.3.1a - Explain the function of nouns, pronouns, verbs, adjectives, and adverbs in general and their functions in particular sentences.

Communication Skill

> The communication skill related to the lesson is identifying nouns and pronouns in reading text. The students will be required to identify pronouns and nouns during instruction and when completing assessment.

Informal Assessment

> I will be informally assessing the students when I ask them to write a sentence on the SMART Board.

Formal Assessment

> The students will complete a formal assessment related to the knowledge of nouns and pronouns, which will require students to identify and write sentences using nouns and pronouns.

Lesson 2

Objective

The objective of the lesson is for the students to read grade appropriate articles and recognize nouns and pronouns.

Educational Standard

Literacy.L.3.1a - Explain the function of nouns, pronouns, verbs, adjectives, and adverbs in general and their functions in particular sentences.

Communication Skill

The communication skill related to the lesson is identifying nouns and pronouns in reading text. The students will be required to identify pronouns and nouns during instruction and when completing assessment.

Informal Assessment

I will be informally assessing the students when reading together, identifying nouns and pronouns, and answering questions.

Formal Assessment

The students will be required to complete a worksheet involving reading short passages and identifying nouns and pronouns.

Lesson 3

Objective

The objectives of the lesson are to understand the function of verb, adjectives, and adverbs, identify verb, adjectives, and adverbs, and write sentences using verb, adjectives, and adverbs.

Educational Standard

Literacy.L.3.1a - Explain the function of nouns, pronouns, verbs, adjectives, and adverbs in general and their functions in particular sentences.

Communication Skill

The communication skill related to the lesson is identifying verb, adjectives, and adverbs in reading text. The students will be required to identify verb, adjectives, and adverbs during instruction and when completing assessment.

Informal Assessment

I will be informally assessing the students when I ask them to write a sentence on the SMART Board.

A jeopardy game will be conducted testing students knowledge on nouns, pronouns, adjectives, verbs, and adverbs, and I will be informally assessing students' performance.

Formal Assessment

The students will complete a formal assessment related to the knowledge of adjectives, verbs, and adverbs, which will require students to identify and write sentences using adjectives, verbs, and adverbs.

Lesson 4

Objective

The objective of the lesson is for the students to write a short essay using nouns, pronouns, verbs, adjectives, and adverbs and be able to recognize them.

Educational Standard

Literacy.L.3.1a - Explain the function of nouns, pronouns, verbs, adjectives, and adverbs in general and their functions in particular sentences.

Communication Skill

The communication skill related to the lesson is identifying nouns, pronouns, verbs, adjectives, and adverbs in reading text. The students will be required to identify nouns, pronouns, verbs, adjectives, and adverbs during instruction and when completing assessment.

Informal Assessment

As a class, the students will be looking at a short story and identifying nouns, pronouns, verbs, adjectives, and adverbs; the students will be observed on performance.

Formal Assessment

The students will write a short story on a prompt in which the students will be required to use and underline nouns, pronouns, verbs, adjectives, and adverbs.

This page is intentionally left blank.

Chapter 8 – Learning Theories

edTPA® tasks require candidates to incorporate, justify, and reference theories and research for planning, instructing, and assessing students. Making a strong connection to theories and research will give candidates a better chance at a higher score. The purpose of this chapter is to inform candidates of some common learning theories and research along with show connection to special education applications. The information included in this chapter is at a high-level; candidates are encouraged to conduct additional research to learn more detail information regarding the theories and research. In addition, the theories and research mentioned in this chapter are only few of many available for candidates to include in the edTPA®.

Learning Theory 1

Theorist – Jean Piaget

Concept/Idea – Scheme, Schemes, & Schema

Definition – Organized ways of making sense of experiences, information, and concepts along with mental systems or categories of perception and experiences.

Example for Special Education – The candidate will have the students learn the basic elements of a sentence. The candidate will conduct multiple activities to ensure students are learning the elements of a sentence. The schema is a stored, so in the future, when asked to write sentences, the students will include the basic elements of a sentence.

Learning Theory 2

Theorist – Jean Piaget

Concept/Idea – Developmental Stages

Definition – Children move through four different stages (sensorimotor, preoperational, concrete operational, and formal operational) of cognitive development roughly at the same age.

Example for Special Education – Speical education teachers will not have or expect students to complete activities that are not grade appropriate. The candidate will use this theory when engaging with students to ensure they are accomplishing specific age group standards.

Learning Theory 3

Theorist – Lev Vygotsky

Concept/Idea – Zone of Proximal Development/Scaffolding

Definition – Zone of Proximal Development states that students can master a task if given appropriate help and support. Scaffolding is when teachers adds supports for students in order to enhance learning.

Example for Special Education – The candidate can show how to use the Hamburger Method to writing a paragraph prior to having the students complete the tasks. Moreover, the teacher can teach the Hamburger Method step by step using anchor charts for the students to master the task of writing a paragraph.

Learning Theory 4

Theorist – Lee Vygotsky

Concept/Idea – Importance of Language

Definition – Language develops from social interactions, and language is a great tool in the learning process. Discussing a problem audibly, internally, or with a partner can support students in the learning process.

Example for Special Education – The candidate can have the students verbally cite the steps for solving a word problem.

Learning Theory 5

Theorist – J.A. Adams

Concept/Idea – Closed Loop Theory

Definition – Feedback guides learning a motor skill. Memory trace selects and initiates given movement plan. Perceptual trace compares movement in progress with correct memory of the movement.

Example for Special Education – The candidate can have students perform same exact movement repeatedly to one accurate end point.

Learning Theory 6

Theorist – Jerome Bruner

Concept/Idea – Spiral Curriculum

Definition – Learning is distributed over time rather than being condensed in shorter periods.

Example for Special Education – The candidate can have the students learn simple addition and subtraction facts, which require memorization. Then, the students can go into complex addition and subtraction, which require them to use knowledge of the facts they have memorized. The students are using information overtime.

Learning Theory 7

Theorist – Allan Paivio

Concept/Idea – Dual Coding

Definition – There are two cognitive subsystems, one specialized for the representation and processing of nonverbal objects/events, and the other specialized for dealing with language.

Example for Special Education – The candidate can verbally teach the students how to solve for x in a linear equation, but also show the students each individual step and break it down on a whiteboard.

Learning Theory 8

Theorist – Vygotsky, Piaget, Wertsch, John-Steiner, & Mahn

Concept/Idea – Learners construct their own knowledge

Definition – Students construct their own knowledge and understanding while engaging in learning.

Example for Special Education – The candidate can have students write a paragraph that focuses on personal experience, but also include elements of learning within the paragraph.

Learning Theory 9

Theorist – Vygotsky, Piaget, Wertsch, John-Steiner, & Mahn

Concept/Idea – Social interactions important in the process of acquiring knowledge

Definition – Using language as a tool to make sense of and learn about the worlds.

Example for Special Education – The candidate can have the students engage in group activity in which students will have to use communication skills.

Learning Theory 10

Theorist – Benjamin Bloom

Concept/Idea – Cognitive Thinking

Definition – Promote higher forms of thinking in education, such as analyzing and evaluating rather than just memorizing. The six basic objectives are knowledge, comprehension, application, analysis, synthesis, and evaluation.

Example for Special Education – The candidate can have students recall previous acquired knowledge before starting a lesson, which is linked to knowledge. The candidate can explain the Hamburger Method to explain how to write a paragraph, which is linked to comprehension. Then, the candidate can have the students use Hamburger Method to write a paragraph, which is linked to application.

Learning Theory 11

Theorist – Albert Bandura

Concept/Idea – Observational Learning

Definition – Learning by observation, imitation of others, and direct instruction.

Example for Special Education – The candidate can show students how to perform the steps to solving for variable in a linear equation and have students perform the same activity.

Learning Theory 12

Theorist – Urie Bronfenbrenner

Concept/Idea – Bioecological Model of Development

Definition – Interactions between the individual and their environment shape each person's development: process, person, context, and time.

Example for Special Education – The candidate can have the students develop a song that focuses on counting. Students are open to include what they desire.

Learning Theory Tip 1

> Make sure that details are provided about the theories, but also how the theories are connected to the learning tasks. Some candidates make general statement about the theories with no strong connection on how the theories are related to the learning tasks.

Learning Theory Tip 2

> When edTPA® prompts ask to reference theories and research, make sure to include at least two theories. The more theories/research included and properly explained in detail will result in a higher score.

This page is intentionally left blank.

Chapter 9 – Generalization, Maintenance, and Self-Directed

Special Education edTPA® require candidates to develop plans that move the focus learner toward generalization, maintenance, and/or self-directed use of knowledge and skills.

Generalization

Generalization is a key component in the learning process. Generalization is the ability to finish a task, perform an activity, or show a behavior across settings, with different individuals, and at different times. Research has shown that students with learning disabilities are more likely to have difficulty transferring their skills to a different setting from the one in which it was learned. In addition, generalization is a critical component in ensuring that the students have mastered the skills being taught.

Generalization Example 1

A teacher is having her students learn how to count money. She uses fake money to engage the students in counting money. Then, the teacher has the students use real money to count money. By first using fake money and then real money, the teacher is having her students generalize the skill of counting money in different settings.

Generalization Example 2

The students will learn how to add and subtract within 20s. Then, the teacher will have the students complete word problems that involve adding and subtracting within 20s. The students acquire knowledge of adding and subtracting within 20s and then use the skill in different setting (solving word problems). Therefore, students are generalizing the skill of adding and subtracting within 20s.

Maintenance

Maintenance is another critical component in the learning process that ensures that students are able to retain knowledge and skills. Maintenance is when students continue to practice a skill that they have previously acquired in order to retain the skill. From a behavior perspective, maintenance is linked to how learners' behavior is self-sustained over time.

Maintenance Example 1

Prior to starting a lesson, the teacher informs the students that they have to raise their hand to speak. This approach is taken in all lessons of the learning segment. By having the students raise their hand to speak in all lessons, the behavior is self-sustained over time.

Maintenance Example 2

After teaching the students nouns, pronouns, verbs, adverbs, and adjectives, the teacher has the students play a jeopardy game to test knowledge. Then, the teacher has the students work in pairs to complete a worksheet assignment on nouns, pronouns, verbs, adverbs, and adjectives. In addition, the teacher requires the students to write a short essay and underline all the nouns, pronouns, verbs, adverbs, and adjectives used in the short essay. The teacher is having the students continue to practice the skill of recognizing nouns, pronouns, verbs, adverbs, and adjectives, so the teacher is taking a method to support students in maintaining knowledge.

Self-Directed

Self-directed is focused on learners becoming more independent in the learning process. This involves teaching students to modify and regulate their own behavior without external control and allow them to be more involved in their own learning. In addition, self-directed can also involve the students independently finding their mistakes or monitoring their progress in the learning process.

Self-Directed Example 1

The teacher has the students complete a math worksheet relating to solving for a variable for linear equations. After the students complete the worksheet, the teacher provides the answer keys. The students are required to correct their steps to questions that were incorrect.

Self-Directed Example 2

When the teacher asks check for understanding questions and the students are incorrect, the teacher will ask follow up questions to elicit the correct answers. This approach will support the students to independently find their mistakes and reach the correct answers.

Planned Support

Planned supports are representations, scaffolds, and pedagogical strategies to help students with generalization, maintenance, and independence. Some examples of planned support include:

- anchor charts
- videos
- questioning
- modeling
- repetition
- class discussion
- flashcards
- flowcharts

edTPA® Requirements of Generalization, Maintenance, and Self-Directed

This section explains the requirements that are related to generalization, maintenance, and self-directed related to Special Education edTPA®.

Task 1

- lesson plans have to incorporate activities to allow students to generalize, maintain, and/or self-direct use of knowledge and skills
- commentary prompt includes explaining how the candidates help the focus learner to generalize, maintain, or self-manage the knowledge, skills, and planned supported related to the learning goal
- commentary prompt includes explaining how supports assist the focus learner in acquiring, maintaining, and/or generalizing the communication skill

Task 2

- commentary prompt includes how strategies were used to move the focus learner toward independently starting and/or maintaining active engagement
- commentary prompt includes how focus learner was involved in self-evaluation and self-correction
- commentary prompt includes how instructional strategies, planned supports and/or materials involved a self-directed learning strategy
- commentary prompt involves documenting changes that move the focus learner toward better maintaining or generalizing knowledge and/or skills

Task 3

- commentary prompt includes explaining how planned supports were provided to help the focus learner to generalize and/or maintain the communication skill

Chapter 10 - Explanation of Planning Commentary

Apart of Task 1 is to complete the planning commentary prompts, which are related to the lesson plans, instructional materials, and assessments developed for the learning segment. The responses on the commentary prompts play a significant factor in the scores' candidates receive. Providing detail, clear, and through responses will show graders a candidate who is competent in planning instruction.

Due to copyright laws, this book will not include the prompts from the edTPA® handbook. Instead, a description of the prompts are written. The candidates are recommended to have a copy of the assessment handbook when reviewing this chapter.

This chapter covers the following:

- Alignment of Learning Goal, Standard, Lesson Objectives, and Planned Supports
- Knowledge of Focus Learner to Inform Teaching of the Learning Segment
- Supporting Learning
- Supporting the Focus Learner's Use of Expressive/Receptive Communication
- Monitoring Learning

Alignment of Learning Goal, Standard, Lesson Objectives, and Planned Supports

Part A: Complete the table below.

Learning Goal:		
Relevant Standard:		
Lesson	Lesson Objective	Planned Supports to Address Learning Goal
Lesson 1		
Lesson 2		
Lesson 3		
Lesson 4		
Lesson 5		

Explanation: The candidates need to directly and clearly state the learning goal and document one standard related to the learning goal. Each lesson plan can only have one measurable objective.

Alignment of Learning Goal, Standard, Lesson Objectives, and Planned Support Tip 1

> For planned supports, try not to include the same supports for each lesson plan. Include various types of supports to increase chances of getting a higher score. In addition, the supports that will be used need to target the focus learner's learning disabilities.

Alignment of Learning Goal, Standard, Lesson Objectives, and Planned Support Tip 2

> For Special Education edTPA®, the candidates are required to select only one standard, so they have to make sure the standard is applicable to all the lessons in the learning segment.

Part B: The prompt ask to explain how the learning goal and planned supports align with IEP goal, explain how the planned supports align with the learning goal, or how learning goal and planned supports align with focus learner's IEP.

Explanation: The key is to document all the planned supports and explain how there are linked to the learning goal or IEP goal. Best way to respond to this is with bullet points. Don't just summarize the planned support; explain how the support is linked to acquiring knowledge related to the learning goal.

Alignment of Learning Goal, Standard, Lesson Objectives, and Planned Support Tip 3

> Some candidates copy paste information from focus learner's IEP for this prompt, which is not the best approach. The purpose is to document the planned supports and make connection to how it helps the learning goal and/or IEP.

Part C: Document any special accommodations or modifications in the learning environment, instruction or assessments required by IEP.

Explanation: The candidates only need to document accommodations or modifications that impact the edTPA® lesson plans. If necessary, the candidates can document "not applicable." Don't assume that a response is absolutely necessary here; this is optional.

Part D: Explain how the lesson plans build on each other along with tasks that help students achieve IEP goals, standards, and the learning goal. The prompt also asks to make connections between focus learner's prior learning and experiences to new learning.

Explanation: The best way to respond to this prompt is to have one paragraph per lesson plan. In each paragraph, start by discussing how the learning activities help develop the focus learner to achieve IEP goals, standards, and/or the learning goal. Also, make the connections between focus learner's prior learning and experiences and new learning for the learning goal. Additional information that needs to be included in each successive paragraph is how the lesson is connected to the previous lesson.

Alignment of Learning Goal, Standard, Lesson Objectives, and Planned Support Tip 4

> This prompt does not require candidates to summarize the lesson plans. The purpose of the prompt is to document how tasks help develop competencies. Use keywords from the prompt, such as "develop," "standards," "sequenced," "learning goal," and "build."

Alignment of Learning Goal, Standard, Lesson Objectives, and Planned Support Tip 5

> In each paragraph, the candidates have to discuss lesson objective, learning tasks, materials, and planned supports. Discussing all four aspects in each paragraph will increase chances of getting a higher score.

Knowledge of Focus Learner to Inform Teaching of the Learning Segment

Part A: Discuss prior knowledge and experiences related to the learning goal. Indicate current focus student's knowledge, activities he/she can perform, and knowledge/skills still acquiring.

Explanation: The best way to respond is discuss what the focus student know, what he/she can do, and what he/she are still learning to do. Information discussed in this prompt need to link back to the learning goal. Candidates can discuss experiences of the focus learner that relate to the lesson objectives and learning goal.

Knowledge of Focus Learner to Inform Teaching of the Learning Segment Tip 1

> The key here is to link responses to what the focus learner know, what he/she can do, and what he/she are still learning to do back to the learning goal.

Knowledge of Focus Learner to Inform Teaching of the Learning Segment Tip 2

Many candidates don't know that they can reference the baseline data obtain for the focus learner in this prompt.

Part B: Discus the focus learner's social and emotional development.

Explanation: The purpose of this response is to provide information about the focus learner related to impulse control, social interaction, and expressing feelings. Discuss how the focus learner interacts with peers and teachers.

Part C: Discuss the focus learner's personal, family, cultural, and community assets.

Explanation: In this prompt, the candidates need to address all four aspects: personal, family, cultural, and community assets. Best approach is to have one paragraph for each asset. For personal asset, discuss the interests, knowledge, and everyday experiences. Family asset includes parents' employment, number of siblings, and support system provided. For cultural asset, think about traditions, language, dialects, and worldviews that the focus learner bring to the classroom. For community asset, discuss where the focus learner lives, community events, and community resources.

Knowledge of Focus Learner to Inform Teaching of the Learning Segment Tip 1

Candidates tend to struggle in connecting to personal, family, cultural, and community assets. Some candidates can't address all four assets. The prompt requires to address all four assets, so if candidates struggle, the best approach is to make stuff up and provide as much detail. Better to make stuff up in detail than keep the prompt unanswered.

Part D: Discuss any other information about the focus learner that impact instructional planning.

Explanation: Only document information about the focus learner that impacts the lesson plans submitted for edTPA®. Don't assume that a response is absolutely necessary here; this is optional.

Supporting Learning

Part A: Discuss how the learning activities, materials, and planned supports address the focus learner's needs and capitalize on strengths and interests.

Explanation: The following can be discussed in this prompt:

- how learning activities, materials, and/or planned supports address student's needs
- how learning activities, materials, and/or planned supports address student's interests
- how learning activities, materials, and/or planned supports address student's strengths

Part B: Discuss how learning activities, materials, and/or planned supports challenged the focus learner.

Explanation: The key is to explain how the focus learner will be challenged to acquire knowledge related to the objectives and learning goal. Some planned supports include equipment, rules, timers, peer support, graphic organizers, anchor charts, instructional cues, and videos.

Part C: Explain the reason for selecting the learning activities, materials, and planned supports in the learning segment.

Explanation: Part A was more related to describing the learning activities, materials, and planned supports, but in this prompt, candidates need to explain why these were selected. The candidates can link it back to strengths, interests, needs, research, and/or theories.

Supporting Students' Special Education Learning Tip 1

> Candidates need to make connection to research and theories in this prompt. This requirement is missed by many students as they fail to write in good detail the connection of learning tasks and materials to theories and research. Not referencing theories and/or research will result in a lower score.

Part D: Explain how the focus learner will generalize, maintain, or self-manage the knowledge, skills, and planned supports.

Explanation: Don't assume that all three (generalize, maintain, or self-manage) need to be discuss. Select the ones that is/are most relevant to the lessons. See Chapter 9 for more information on generalize, maintain, or self-manage the knowledge, skills, and planned supports.

Supporting the Focus Learner's Use of Expressive/Receptive Communication

Part A: Identify one communication skill related to the learning goal that the focus learner will need to use.

Explanation: One sentence response should suffice for this prompt. (ex. The communication skill that will be used to help the focus learner achieve the learning goal is _____.)

Supporting the Focus Learner's Use of Expressive/Receptive Communication Tip 1

> Some candidates document more than one communication skill for each lesson plan. The prompt only requires documenting one communication skill for the learning goal widely used in the learning segment.

Part B: Explain how the focus learner will be supported to use the communication skill. In addition, explain how the supports will assist the focus learner in acquiring, maintaining, and/or generalizing the communication skill.

Explanation: Use bullet point format to document the planned supports and explain how it will help students use the communication skill. In addition, make sure to mention how the focus learner will acquire, maintain, and/or generalize the communication skill. Planned supports include learning environment, instructional strategies, learning tasks, materials, accommodations, assistive technology, prompts, and modifications.

Monitoring Learning

Part A: Describe how assessments, daily assessment records, and baseline data will allow the focus learner to acquire knowledge related to the learning goal and objectives. In addition, discuss the level of support and challenge appropriate for the focus learner's needs.

Explanation: The best way to respond to this prompt is have three paragraphs: one for assessments, one for daily assessment records, and one for baseline data.

Monitoring Student Learning Tip 1

> Don't just summarize the assessments that will be used in the learning segment. The key is to make the connection on how the assessment shows evidence of the focus learner acquiring knowledge related to the learning goal and objectives.

Part B: Discuss how the focus learner will monitor his/her own learning progress.

Explanation: To increase chances of a higher score, each lesson needs to incorporate how the focus learner will monitor his/her own learning progress. The best way to respond to this prompt is one paragraph per lesson plan explaining how the focus learner will be involved in monitoring progress.

This page is intentionally left blank.

Chapter 11 - Explanation of Instruction Commentary

Apart of Task 2 is to complete the instruction commentary prompts, which are related to how candidates provided instruction to the students during the learning segment. The responses on the commentary prompts play a significant factor in the scores' candidate receive. Providing detail, clear, and through responses will show graders a candidate who is competent in instructing.

Due to copyright laws, this book will not include the prompts from the edTPA® handbook. Instead, a description of the prompt is written. The candidates are recommended to have a copy of the assessment handbook when reviewing this chapter.

This chapter covers the following:

- Promoting a Positive Learning Environment
- Engaging and Motivating the Focus Learner
- Deepening Learning
- Supporting Teaching and Learning
- Analyzing Teaching

Instruction Commentary Tip 1

> The point of submitting the video(s) is to reference examples from the video(s). Try to avoid using examples that are not included in the video. Find examples from the video(s) to document in the commentary prompts. Candidates can use the same time references in multiple prompts.

Instruction Commentary Tip 2

> A requirement of the instruction commentary is to time reference the video clip(s). The best way to time reference the video clip(s) is the following: (Clip 1: Timestamp: 4:33). The time reference is best placed at the end of the sentence.

Question 1: Document the lesson or lessons shown in the clip(s). Describe any changes made during instruction and reasons for those changes.

Explanation: A simple sentence will surface here (ex. Clip 1 shows lesson X.). If any changes are made, document those with the reasons for making the changes during instruction.

Question 2: Document any information to understand the learning environment or interactions. Describe the focus learner in the video clip(s).

Explanation: If there is any additional information needed to understand the environment or interactions, document it in this prompt. If instruction is done one-on-one, this is a good place to explain the reason for taking this approach. Otherwise, the candidates can indicate "not applicable." Also, make sure to describe the clothing and position of the focus learner in the video clip(s).

Promoting a Positive Learning Environment

Part A: Explain how instruction showed respect for and rapport for all learners.

Explanation: The candidates can respond in two ways:

-   one paragraph for respect and one paragraph for rapport
-   bullet points for each instance/example from the video(s) that show respect for and rapport for all learners

The best approach is to include examples from the video(s). Moreover, recommendation is to include at least two examples for providing respect for and rapport for all learners. So, a total of at least four examples are recommended.

The following are some ways to show rapport for all learners:

-   learn to call students by first name
-   learn something about students' interests, hobbies, and aspirations
-   create and use personally relevant class examples
-   explain the purpose of learning
-   interact more, lecture less
-   positive feedback for correct responses
-   be enthusiastic about teaching and passionate
-   make eye contact with each student
-   be respectful
-   don't forget to smile

Part B: Explain how a positive learning environment that supported and challenged the focus learner to achieve the learning goal was established. Explain how the focus learner was directed toward self-determination.

Explanation: The best way to respond to this prompt is by using bullet point format explaining instances from the video clip(s) showing an environment that is supportive and challenging along with moving the focus learner to self-determination.

Engaging and Motivating the Focus Learner

Part A: Explain how the strategies engaged and motivated the focus learner to develop and apply knowledge related to the learning goal.

Explanation: Some examples of instructional strategies include direct modeling, lecture strategy, individualized instruction, task teaching, cooperative learning, problem solving, peer teaching strategy, think-pair-share activities, repetition, scaffolding, creative thinking, question strategy, and simulations. Make the connection on how the focus learner was engaged and motivated to learn due to the strategies used in the learning segment.

Part B: Explain how instruction was linked to focus learner's prior knowledge and personal, family, cultural, and/or community assets.

Explanation: In this response, prior knowledge has to be discussed along with at least one asset. To obtain a higher score, the candidates need to time reference the example(s) from the video(s).

Part C: Discuss how the strategies used moved the focus learner toward independently initiating and/or maintaining engagement.

Explanation: Special Education edTPA® emphasizes on getting focus learner to independently engage in learning. In this prompt, include strategies and tasks that involve the focus learner to be independent in the learning process.

Deepening Learning

Part A: Explain how the focus learner's responses were elicited and how feedback was provided to improve focus learner's performance related to the learning goal.

Explanation: Candidates need to discuss the steps and strategies taken to elicit the focus learner's responses during instruction. Moreover, the candidates need to explain how they provided feedback to the focus learner to develop competencies related to the learning goal. For example, some candidates give feedback right after a student completes an activity. Others give feedback after everyone has completed or after 15 minutes into the lesson by pausing activity and discussing feedback. Remember to reference the video clip(s).

Part B: Discuss opportunities provided to the focus learner to apply feedback.

Explanation: The best way to respond to this prompt is in bullet point format explaining all instances in the video(s) where the student was able to apply the feedback provided during instruction.

Part C: Describe how the focus learner was moved toward self-evaluation and self-correction.

Explanation: Self-evaluation is having the focus learner monitor his/her progress during instruction. Self-correction is giving the focus learner multiple attempts to correct himself or herself. Discuss at least 2 examples from the video that move the focus learner toward self-evaluation and self-correction.

Supporting Teaching and Learning

Part A: Explain how materials, planned supports, and instructional strategies helped the focus learner progress toward the objectives. Discuss how they reflected the learner's development, age, strengths, and needs.

Explanation: There are two ways the candidates can respond to this prompt:

- one paragraph for materials, planned supports, and instructional strategies
- bullet point format discussing materials, planned supports, and instructional strategies

In the response, the candidates need to explain how the focus learner progressed toward the lesson objectives. Do not just provide summary of what was used. A connection to the focus learner progressing toward objectives is necessary.

Part B: Discuss how the materials, planned supports, and/or instructional strategies prompted a self-directed learning strategy for the learning goal.

Explanation: Self-directed learning strategy is getting learners to modify and regulate their own behavior without teacher involvement and allow them to become active participants in their own learning. Candidates need to discuss few examples from the video clip(s) of how a self-directed learning strategy was employed in the lesson(s).

Analyzing Teaching

Part A: Document changes to instruction and missed opportunities to better support the focus student.

Explanation: Candidates should address changes to instruction and missed opportunities that target the focus learner to improve on performance and/or move the focus learner toward maintained, generalized, or self-directed use of knowledge.

Analyzing Teaching – Tip 1

> To increase chances of getting more points, the changes candidates discuss have to be seen in the video clip(s) submitted.

Part B: Explain why the recommended changes are necessary to foster improvement in focus learner's learning.

Explanation: Respond to this prompt with bullet point format explaining why the changes are needed to ensure better learning. Each recommended change must be supported by evidence of focus learner's learning, and research and/or theories. Research and/or theories references are mandatory in this prompt.

This page is intentionally left blank.

Chapter 12 - Explanation of Assessment Commentary

Apart of Task 3 is to complete the assessment commentary prompts, which are related to how candidates assessed the focus learner during the learning segment. The responses on the commentary prompts play a significant factor in the scores' candidates receive. Providing detail, clear, and through responses will show graders a candidate who is competent in assessing students.

Due to copyright laws, this book will not include the prompts from the edTPA® handbook. Instead, a description of the prompt is written. The candidates are recommended to have a copy of the assessment handbook when reviewing this chapter.

This chapter covers the following:

- Analyzing the Focus Learner's Performance
- Feedback to Guide Further Learning
- Evidence of Use of the Expressive/Receptive Communication Skill
- Using Assessment to Inform Instruction

Analysis Students Learning

Part A: Document the learning objectives measured by each daily assessment records for analysis.

Explanation: Only document the objectives related to the daily assessment records. The candidates can use bullet point format to clearly and directly respond to the prompt. There is no need to explain the lesson activities or summarize the lessons in this prompt.

Part B: Document any changes made to assessment related to the work sample, daily assessment records, and/or lesson objectives from what was described in the lesson plans. Explain the reason for making the changes.

Explanation: This is an optional prompt. If no changes exist, document "not applicable."

Part C: If the work sample is from Task 2 video, document the time reference and identify the focus learner in the video.

Explanation: This is an optional prompt. If video is not used for the work sample, document "not applicable."

Part D: Summarize by using paragraphs or construct a table showing the focus learner's progress toward the learning goal.

Explanation: The graders are looking for how the focus learner's developed knowledge related to the learning goal. All objectives need to be addressed in this prompt.

Analysis Students Learning Tip 1

> The candidates sometimes only discuss the assessment that was selected for Task 3. However, the graders are looking for summary of all objectives in the learning segment.

Part E: Analyze the focus learner's performance based on strengths and needs. Discuss any error analysis along with planned supports provided to the focus learner.

Explanation: The best way to respond is two paragraphs: one for strengths and one for needs. Using the information in Part D and sample work, the candidates need to discuss strengths and needs of the focus learner. In addition, include a paragraph on the planned supports provided to the focus learner.

Part F: Discuss effectiveness of the planned supports.

Explanation: Explain how the planned supports used were supportive or not supportive in the focus learner's progression toward the learning goal. The candidates can respond in bullet point format and explain the effectiveness or ineffectiveness of the planned supports.

Feedback to Guide Further Learning

Part A: Identify the format in which feedback was submitted.

Explanation: Simply select one of the options provided in the commentary prompt.

Part B: Explain how the feedback (including error prevention) provided to the focus learner connect to his/her strengths and needs relative to the learning goal.

Explanation: The best way to respond to this prompt is using one paragraph for strengths and one paragraph for needs. Directly state how the feedback is related to the focus learner's strengths and needs.

Part C: Discuss how the focus learner will be supported to comprehend and apply feedback provided.

Explanation: Respond to this prompt by addressing the following:

- explaining how to support students in understanding feedback
- using the feedback within the learning segment
- using the feedback to develop the students in future learning activities

Evidence of Use of the Expressive/Receptive Communication Skill

Part A: Explain and give examples of students using communication skill to participate or to show learning relative to the learning goal.

Explanation: The candidates need to provide concrete examples of the focus learner using communication skills. When discussing examples, references need to be made from one or more of the following sources:

- video clip(s) submitted for Task 2 – must provide time-stamp references.
- submit extra video named "Communication Use" with no more than 5 minutes
- student's work sample

Part B: Discuss how planned supports for expressive/receptive communication built on focus learner's strengths and needs.

Explanation: To maximize score, candidates want to discuss both expressive communication and receptive communication. The candidates can respond by having one paragraph for expressive communication and one paragraph for receptive communication. In each paragraph, the strengths and needs have to be discussed. In addition, including references from source(s) is a good idea.

Part C: Describe how the planned supports help the focus learner generalize and/or maintain communication skill.

Explanation: The best way to respond to this prompt is with bullet points. Include 2-3 examples of how the supports help the focus learner generalize and/or maintain communication skill.

Using Assessment to Inform Instruction

Part A: Describe next steps for instruction to further learning.

Explanation: In this response, indicate 3-4 next steps for instruction to improve or continue learning. Provide explanations as to why the next steps are necessary based on focus learner's performance and research/theories.

Part B: Document implications for the focus learner's IEP goals and/or curriculum.

Explanation: In this response, avoid documenting "not applicable." Here the graders want to see how candidates can recommend changes to focus learner's IEP goals and/or curriculum based on performance.

Chapter 13 - Special Education edTPA® Example ®

The Special Education edTPA® requires the candidates to show and develop understanding in teaching students with learning disabilities. The candidates will identify one learning goal and develop lesson plans to build knowledge to achieve the learning goal.

The goal of the Special Education edTPA® is for the candidates to show readiness to teach students with multiple learning disabilities. Successful candidates can develop knowledge of subject matter, content standards, and subject-specific pedagogy along with meet the needs of focus student. Moreover, candidates can incorporate research and theories regarding how students learn.

The chapter covers the following:

- Task 1: Part A – Context for Learning Information
- Task 1: Part B – Lesson Plans for Learning Segment
- Task 1: Part C – Instructional Materials
- Task 1: Part D – Assessments and/or Data Collection Procedures
- Task 1: Part E – Planning Commentary
- Task 2: Part A – Video Clips
- Task 2: Part B – Instruction Commentary
- Task 3: Part A – Work Sample
- Task 3: Part B – Completed Daily Assessment Records and Baseline Data
- Task 3: Part C – Evidence of Feedback
- Task 3: Part D – Assessment Commentary

This chapter includes a complete edTPA® portfolio for the Special Education subject area. Since this is a real edTPA, there are some mistakes within the portfolio along with some grammar, punctuation, and usage errors. Nonetheless, this still is considered a very strong edTPA® portfolio. The purpose of providing an authentic edTPA® portfolio is to show candidates how to develop successful portfolios.

This page is intentionally left blank.

Task 1 Part A – Special Education Context for Learning Information

About the Placement and Your Role in the Focus Learner's Instruction

Context for Learning

Part A

- This is a third-grade classroom in an elementary school. Instruction will take place in a regular classroom.
- The school is located in a city.
- I teach all academic subjects plus support the student in behavioral plans.
- Each day the focus learner will devote 50 minutes to achieve the learning goal. Instruction will take place in the morning.
- The primary language of the focus learner is Spanish.

Part B

No additional district, school, or cooperating teacher requirements that impact instruction.

Part C

No additional textbook or instructional program required in this learning segment.

Part D

There are six students involved in the learning segment. Four students have IEPs, and two are general education learners.

About the Focus Learner

1. Age – 9 years ago
2. Gender – Male
3. Grade Level – 3rd Grade
4. Language – Bilingual in English and Spanish
5. ADHD, Autism, and Auditory Processing Disorder
6. Augmentative or Alternative Communication – Not applicable
7. Behavioral Plans – The student has issues with staying focused along with shouting unnecessarily. The student can also be rude to peers. Plans include reminding the student to stay focused. When engaged in activities, the student is reminded to be respectful.

This page is intentionally left blank.

Task 1 Part B – Lesson Plans For Learning Segment

Lesson One

Lesson Title: Nouns

Grade Level: 3rd Grade Instruction

Learning Goal

The learning goal is for the focus learner to understand, recognize, and use pronouns, nouns, verbs, adjectives, and adverbs when reading and writing.

Educational Standard

CCSS.ELA-Literacy.L.3.1.a Explain the function of nouns, pronouns, verbs, adjectives, and adverbs in general and their functions in particular sentences.

Objective

The objective is for the students to read text and to complete worksheet related to understanding, identifying, and using nouns.

Instructional Materials/Resources

The following are materials/resources used during instruction:

- anchor charts
- video
- Smart Board
- Reading Text

Instructional Procedures (detail steps to instruction)

Step 1

I will welcome the students to the classroom, and I will inform them about the lesson objective. I will inform the students that we will be learning about nouns, which is one of the key parts of speech.

Step 2

I will remind the students about raising hands when wanting to speak. I will also remind the students to be respectful to one another along with using an indoor voice.

Step 3

I will introduce the definition of a noun using an anchor chart. I will explain to them what consist of a noun. I will provide examples of nouns. In addition, I will provide suggestions on how to determine the noun of a sentence.

Step 4

I will call on students to repeat the definition of a noun along with provide examples of nouns.

Step 5

I will also show the students a video about the definition of a noun along with several examples.

Step 6

On the Smart Board, I will write a sentence, and I will call on one student to identify the noun. I will ask peers to agree or disagree with the student's answer. I will do six examples on the Smart Board.

Step 7

I will have the students read a short informational text and have them underline all the nouns they can find in the text. Once completed, the students will be asked to put away their pencils. I will provide them with a red pen. As a class, we will review the answers.

Step 8

I will recap the learning of the lesson. Then, I will give each student a worksheet related to finding nouns. As the students complete the worksheet independently, I will walk around the classroom to ensure the students are actively working.

Instructional Strategies (what instructional strategies will be used in the lesson)

- Incorporating Technologies
- Repetition
- Check for Understanding

Communication Skill and Planned Supports

The communication skill that will be required in this lesson is selecting the correct noun. The planned supports used in achieving the communication skill are anchor chart, repetition, and video.

Generalization, Maintenance, and/or Self-Directed Use of Knowledge and Skills

The students will acquire knowledge related to noun via direct instruction, video, and in-class activities. The students will be able to generalize the knowledge by identifying nouns in sentences and reading texts.

To maintain skill, the students will practice identifying nouns in multiple ways:

- identifying nouns in sentences written on Smart Board
- reading short informational text and identifying nouns
- completing worksheet identifying nouns

The students will be involved in grading themselves after reading the short informational text and identifying nouns. During in-class activities, if the student is incorrect, he or she will have the opportunity to try again to reach the correct answer.

Assessments (Formal and Informal)

The following are assessments related to this lesson:

- The students will be observed when identifying nouns during in-class activities.
- The students will complete a reading activity in which they will identify nouns.
- The students will complete a worksheet in which they will identify nouns.

Lesson Two

Lesson Title: Pronouns

Grade Level: 3rd Grade Instruction

Learning Goal

The learning goal is for the focus learner to understand, recognize, and use pronouns, nouns, verbs, adjectives, and adverbs when reading and writing.

Educational Standard

CCSS.ELA-Literacy.L.3.1.a Explain the function of nouns, pronouns, verbs, adjectives, and adverbs in general and their functions in particular sentences.

Objective

The objective is for the students to gain knowledge related to pronouns and to show competencies by completing a worksheet related to pronouns.

Instructional Materials/Resources

The following are materials/resources used during instruction:

- anchor charts
- index cards
- Smart Board
- posters

Instructional Procedures (detail steps to instruction)

Step 1

I will welcome the students to the classroom, and I will inform them about the lesson objective. I will inform the students that we will be learning about pronouns, which is one of the key parts of speech.

Step 2

I will remind the students about raising hands when wanting to speak. I will also remind the students to be respectful to one another along with using an indoor voice.

Step 3

I will introduce the definition of pronoun using an anchor chart. I will explain to them what consist of a pronoun. I will provide examples of pronouns. In addition, I will provide suggestions on how to determine the pronoun in a sentence.

Step 4

I will call on students to repeat the definition of a pronoun along with provide examples of pronouns.

Step 5

I will also show the students a poster with a sentence and have them identify the pronoun. On the back of the poster, the answer will be written. I will have two posters to show the students.

Step 6

On the Smart Board, I will write a sentence, and I will call on one student to come up and identify the pronoun. I will ask peers to agree or disagree with the student's answer. I will do six examples on the Smart Board. In few of the sentences, I will have two pronouns for the students to identify.

Step 7

I will do an in-class activity with the students involving using index cards. I will have six index cards; three cards with nouns and three cards with pronouns. The cards will be in a bowl. Each student will pick one card. The students will be asked to think of a sentence using the part of speech written on the selected card. Each student will write his or her sentence on the Smart Board, and the class will identify the part of speech in the sentence. The teacher will start by modeling a sentence on the whiteboard for the students.

Step 8

I will recap the learning of the lesson. Then, I will give each student a worksheet related to finding verbs. As the students complete the worksheet independently, I will walk around the classroom to ensure the students are actively working.

Step 9

Once the students complete the worksheet, the class will go over the correct answers together. I will give the students a red pen to self-grade.

Instructional Strategies (what instructional strategies will be used in the lesson)

- Repetition
- Visual Aids (posters and anchor chart)
- Group Engagement

Communication Skill and Planned Supports

The communication skill that will be required in this lesson is selecting the correct pronoun. The planned supports used in the lesson in achieving the communication skill are anchor charts, repetition, and group activity.

Generalization, Maintenance, and/or Self-Directed Use of Knowledge and Skills

The students will acquire knowledge related to pronouns. The students will be using this knowledge and skill in different environments (paired activity and independent activity). Also, I will include some sentences that have multiple pronouns for students to find, allowing them to generalize the knowledge acquired.

To maintain skill, the students will practice identifying pronouns in multiple ways:

- identifying pronoun(s) in sentences displayed on posters
- identifying and using pronouns during in-class activity
- completing worksheet identifying pronouns

The students will be involved in grading themselves after completing worksheet related to pronouns. During in-class activities, if the student is incorrect, he or she will have the opportunity to try again to reach the correct answer.

Assessments (Formal and Informal)

The following are assessments related to this lesson:

- The students will be observed when identifying pronouns during in-class activities.
- The students will complete a worksheet in which they will identify pronouns.

Lesson Three

Lesson Title: Verbs

Grade Level: 3rd Grade Instruction

Learning Goal

The learning goal is for the focus learner to understand, recognize, and use pronouns, nouns, verbs, adjectives, and adverbs when reading and writing.

Educational Standard

CCSS.ELA-Literacy.L.3.1.a Explain the function of nouns, pronouns, verbs, adjectives, and adverbs in general and their functions in particular sentences.

Objective

The objective is for the students to gain knowledge related to verbs and show competencies by completing a worksheet related to verbs.

Instructional Materials/Resources

The following are materials/resources used during instruction:

- anchor chart
- video
- Smart Board
- Reading Text

Instructional Procedures (detail steps to instruction)

Step 1

I will welcome the students to the classroom, and I will inform them about the lesson objective. I will inform the students that we will be learning about verbs, which is one of the key parts of speech.

Step 2

I will remind the students about raising hands when wanting to speak. I will also remind the students to be respectful to one another along with using an indoor voice.

Step 3

I will introduce the definition of a verb using an anchor chart. I will explain to them what consist of a verb. I will provide examples of verbs. In addition, I will provide suggestions on how to determine the verb in a sentence.

Step 4

I will call on students to repeat the definition of a verb along with provide examples of verbs.

Step 5

I will also show the students a video defining verb along with showing examples of finding verbs in sentences.

Step 6

On the Smart Board, I will write a sentence, and I will call on one student to come up and identify the verb. I will ask peers to agree or disagree with the student's answer. I will do six examples on the Smart Board. In few of the sentences, I will have two verbs for the students to identify.

Step 7

I will have students read a short informational text and have them underline all the verbs they can find in the text. Once completed, the students will be asked to put away their pencils. I will provide them with a red pen. As a class, we will review the answers together.

Step 8

I will recap the learning of the lesson. Then, I will give each student a worksheet related to finding nouns. As the students complete the worksheet independently, I will walk around the classroom to ensure the students are actively working.

Instructional Strategies (what instructional strategies will be used in the lesson)

- Repetition
- Visual Aids (video and anchor chart)
- Group Activity

Communication Skill and Planned Supports

The communication skill that will be required in this lesson is selecting the correct verb. The planned supports used in the lesson to support in achieving the communication skill are anchor charts, repetition, and group activity.

Generalization, Maintenance, and/or Self-Directed Use of Knowledge and Skills

The students will acquire knowledge related to verb. The students will be using this knowledge and skill in different environments (group activity and independent activity). The students will be able to generalize knowledge when they encounter sentences with more than one verb.

To maintain skill, the students will practice identifying verbs in multiple ways:

- identifying verbs in sentence displayed in the video
- reading short informational text and identifying verbs
- completing worksheet identifying verbs

The students will be involved in grading themselves after reading the short informational text and identifying verbs. During in-class activities, if the student is incorrect, he or she will have the opportunity to try again to reach the correct answer.

Assessments (Formal and Informal)

The following are assessments related to this lesson:

- The students will be observed when identifying verbs during in-class activities.
- The students will complete a reading activity in which they will identify verbs.
- The students will complete a worksheet in which they will identify verbs.

Lesson Four

Lesson Title: Adverbs

Grade Level: 3rd Grade Instruction

Learning Goal

The learning goal is for the focus learner to understand, recognize, and use pronouns, nouns, verbs, adjectives, and adverbs when reading and writing.

Educational Standard

CCSS.ELA-Literacy.L.3.1.a Explain the function of nouns, pronouns, verbs, adjectives, and adverbs in general and their functions in particular sentences.

Objective

The objective is for the students to gain knowledge related to adverbs and to show competencies by completing a worksheet related to adverbs.

Instructional Materials/Resources

The following are materials/resources used during instruction:

- anchor chart
- index cards
- Smart Board
- posters

Instructional Procedures (detail steps to instruction)

Step 1

I will welcome the students to the classroom, and I will inform them about the lesson objective. I will inform the students that we will be learning about adverbs, which is one of the key parts of speech.

Step 2

I will remind the students about raising hands when wanting to speak. I will also remind the students to be respectful to one another along with using an indoor voice.

Step 3

I will introduce the definition of an adverb using an anchor chart. I will explain to them what consist of an adverb. I will provide examples of adverbs. In addition, I will provide suggestions on how to determine the adverb in a sentence.

Step 4

I will call on students to repeat the definition of an adverb along with provide examples of adverbs.

Step 5

I will also show the students a poster with a sentence and have them identify the adverb. On the back of the poster, the answer will be written. I will have two posters to show the students.

Step 6

On the Smart Board, I will have a sentence written, and I will call on one student to come up and identify the adverb. I will ask peers to agree or disagree with the student's answer. I will do six examples on the Smart Board.

Step 7

I will do an in-class paired activity involving index cards. Each student will be given one index card, and the students will write a sentence using adverb. Then, the students will exchange the index card and have to identify the adverb.

Step 8

I will repeat Step 7. Students will work with different partners.

Step 9

I will recap the learning of the lesson. Then, I will give each student a worksheet related to finding adverbs. As the students complete the worksheet independently, I will walk around the classroom to ensure the students are actively working.

Step 10

Once the students complete the worksheet, the class will go over the correct answers together. I will give the students a red pen to self-grade.

Instructional Strategies (what instructional strategies will be used in the lesson)

- Visual Aids
- Repetition
- Paired Activity

Communication Skill and Planned Supports

The communication skill that will be required in this lesson is selecting the correct adverb. The planned supports used in the lesson in achieving the communication skill are anchor charts, repetition, and paired activity.

Generalization, Maintenance, and/or Self-Directed Use of Knowledge and Skills

The students will acquire knowledge related to adverbs and examples of adverbs. The students will be using this knowledge and skill in different environments (paired activity and independent activity).

To maintain skill, the students will practice identifying adverbs in multiple ways:

- identifying adverbs in sentences displayed on posters
- identifying and using adverbs during paired activity
- completing worksheet identifying adverbs

The students will be involved in grading themselves after completing worksheet related to adverbs. During in-class activities, if the student is incorrect, he or she will have the opportunity to try again to reach the correct answer.

Assessments (Formal and Informal)

The following are assessments related to this lesson:

- The students will be observed when identifying adverbs during in-class activities.
- The students will complete a worksheet in which they will identify adverbs.

Lesson Five

Lesson Title: Adjectives

Grade Level: 3rd Grade Instruction

Learning Goal

The learning goal is for the focus learner to understand, recognize, and use pronouns, nouns, verbs, adjectives, and adverbs when reading and writing.

Educational Standard

CCSS.ELA-Literacy.L.3.1.a Explain the function of nouns, pronouns, verbs, adjectives, and adverbs in general and their functions in particular sentences.

Objective

The objective is for the students to gain knowledge related to adjectives and to show competencies by completing a worksheet related to adjectives.

Instructional Materials/Resources

The following are materials/resources used during instruction:

- anchor chart
- video
- index cards
- Smart Board
- posters
- sticky notes

Instructional Procedures (detail steps to instruction)

Step 1

I will welcome the students to the classroom, and I will inform them about the lesson objective. I will inform the students that we will be learning about adjectives, which is one of the key parts of speech.

Step 2

I will remind the students about raising hands when wanting to speak. I will also remind the students to be respectful to one another along with using an indoor voice.

Step 3

I will introduce the definition of an adjective using an anchor chart. I will explain to them what consist of an adjective. I will provide examples of adjectives. In addition, I will provide suggestions on how to determine the adjective in a sentence.

Step 4

I will call on students to repeat the definition of an adjective along with provide examples of adjectives.

Step 5

I will also show the students a video defining adjective along with showing examples of finding adjectives in sentences.

Step 6

On the Smart Board, I will write a sentence, and I will call on one student to come up and identify the adjectives. I will ask peers to agree or disagree with the student's answer. I will do six examples on the Smart Board. Some of the sentences will include two adjectives to find.

Step 7

I will do an in-class paired activity involving index cards. Each student will be given one index card, and the students will write a sentence using adjective. Then, the students will exchange the index card and have to identify the adjective.

Step 8

I will repeat Step 7. Students will work with different partners.

Step 9

A poster will be divided into 5 sections for noun, pronoun, verb, adverb, and adjective. I will give each student 2 sticky notes with words, and the students will be required to place the word in the correct section. Then, I will ask the focus learner to see if there are any mistakes that need to be corrected.

Step 10

I will recap the learning of the lesson. Then, I will give each student a worksheet related to finding adjectives, but I will also include questions related to noun, pronoun, verb, and adverb. As the students complete the worksheet independently, I will walk around the classroom to ensure the students are actively working.

Instructional Strategies (what instructional strategies will be used in the lesson)

- Repetition
- Group/Paired Activity
- Technology Integration

Communication Skill and Planned Supports

The communication skill that will be required in this lesson is selecting the correct adjective. The planned supports used in the lesson in achieving the communication skill are anchor chart, repetition, and paired/group activity.

Generalization, Maintenance, and/or Self-Directed Use of Knowledge and Skills

The students will acquire knowledge related to adjectives and examples of adjectives. The students will be using this knowledge and skill in different environments (paired activity and independent activity).

To maintain skill, the students will practice identifying adjectives in multiple ways:

- identifying adjectives in sentence displayed on poster
- identifying and using adjectives during flashcard activity
- completing worksheet identifying adjectives

During in-class activities, if the student is incorrect, he or she will have opportunity to try again to reach the correct answer. I will also have the focus learner review poster with sticky notes to see if there are any mistakes that need to be corrected.

Assessments (Formal and Informal)

The following are assessments related to this lesson:

- The students will be observed when identifying adjectives during in-class activities.
- The students will complete a worksheet in which they will identify adjectives along with nouns, pronouns, verbs, and adverbs.

This page is intentionally left blank.

Lesson 1 – Anchor Chart (Nouns)

Nouns

What are nouns?

- Parts of speech that can be used as the subject of a sentence

- Nouns name a person, place or thing

Example of nouns

snake (thing)   James (person)   house (place)

How to find nouns?

- Look for names, places, and things

- Names and places are sometimes capitalized

Lesson 1 – Video (Nouns)

There is one video used that explains definition of noun along with examples.

Lesson 1 – Smart Board

Playing Soccer

Soccer is played throughout the world. In most places except for the United States, soccer is known as football. The basic concept to soccer is two teams playing with a round ball on a field, and each team attempts to put the ball in the other team's goal. A player called the goalie guards the team's goal. These players are the only ones who can touch the ball with their arms and hands.

The other players move the ball by kicking it. They can also head a ball in the air using their heads, and they can run with the ball by dribbling it by kicking the ball to themselves with short, quick taps. To ensure that all rules are being strictly followed, a referee can call a foul if a player breaks a rule. The referee can give the other team a penalty kick or free kick.

Basic soccer uses inexpensive equipment, making one of the easiest games to play around the world. Many individuals come together and play soccer on a nice stretch of grass. They can use jersey, shorts, socks, cleats, and shin guards. Casually, playing in the neighborhood, tennis shoes can be used instead of shin guards. Cleats assist in gripping the grass so players can run and turn faster. Protecting your ankles and legs are very important when spinning, turning, kicking, and changing directions, and the cleats provide that protection.

Pronouns

What are pronouns?

- Parts of speech that can be used as the subject of a sentence

- Pronoun is a word that is used in place of or stands for a noun

Example of common pronouns

I	You	He	She	It	We	Us	Me
	They	Its	Our	Your	Them		

What is antecedent?

The noun that the pronoun stands for is called the antecedent.

How to find pronouns?

- Remember common pronouns

- Connect the pronoun to the noun that is replaced

Sentence: The butterfly was small and it went into every room in the office before leaving.

Identify the pronoun(s).

Pronoun(s): it (describing the butterfly)

Sentence: The flies were in the sky, and it was night time.

Identify the pronoun(s).

Pronoun(s): it (describing the sky)

noun

pronoun

noun

pronoun

noun

pronoun

Verbs

What are verbs?

- Necessary for a sentence to be complete

- A verb is a word which describes the action in a sentence

Examples of verb

- Juan likes to run.

- I am looking to buy a house.

- My computer broke, so I need to buy a new computer.

How to find verb?

- Think of the verb as the "doing" word

- A sentence will always have a verb to be a complete sentence.

Lesson 3 – Video (Verbs)

There is one video used that explains definition of noun along with verbs.

Lesson 3 – Smart Board

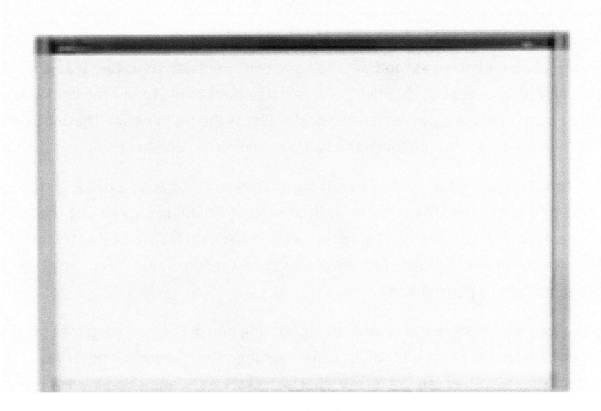

Playing Soccer

Soccer is played throughout the world. In most places except for the United States, soccer is known as football. The basic concept to soccer is two teams playing with a round ball on a field, and each team attempts to put the ball in the other team's goal. A player called the goalie guards the team's goal. These players are the only ones who can touch the ball with their arms and hands.

The other players move the ball by kicking it. They can also head a ball in the air using their heads, and they can run with the ball by dribbling it by kicking the ball to themselves with short, quick taps. To ensure that all rules are being strictly followed, a referee can call a foul if a player breaks a rule. The referee can give the other team a penalty kick or free kick.

Basic soccer uses inexpensive equipment, making one of the easiest games to play around the world. Many individuals come together and play soccer on a nice stretch of grass. They can use jersey, shorts, socks, cleats, and shin guards. Casually, playing in the neighborhood, tennis shoes can be used instead of shin guards. Cleats assist in gripping the grass so players can run and turn faster. Protecting your ankles and legs are very important when spinning, turning, kicking, and changing directions, and the cleats provide that protection.

Adverbs

What are adverbs?

- A word that describes a verb

- An adverb tells us when, where, and how about verbs, adjectives and even other adverbs

Example of adverbs

- The baby carried loudly.

- The brother drove faster than his friend.

- Everyone waited quietly for the news report.

How to find adverbs?

- Look out for words ending in "ing" or "er" or "est"

- Find the verb and see if there is an adjective around the verb

Sentence: He was looking carefully at the window for his dad to come back.

Identify the adverb(s).

Adverb: carefully

Sentence: Walking to the car, he was extremely worried it might rain.

Identify the adverb(s).

Adverb: extremely

Adjectives

What are adjectives?

- An adjective is a word that tells us more about a noun or a pronoun.

- An adjective describes or modifies a noun.

Example of adjectives

large city – red rose – new house – small butterfly – bright, yellow sun

How to find adjectives?

- Adjectives usually answer three questions about the nouns they describe:

  What kind of? - How many? - Which one(s)?

Lesson 5 – Video (Adjectives)

There is one video used that explains definition of adjectives along with examples.

Lesson 5 – Index Cards

Lesson 5 – Smart Board

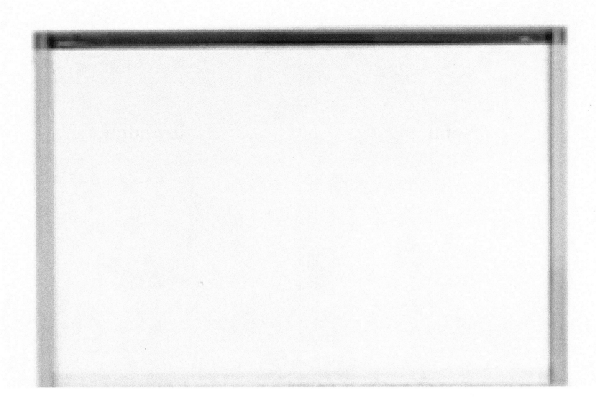

Verb	Adverb	Adjectives

Noun	Pronoun

house   ran   car

soccer   happily   small

ate   drawing   quickly

green   loudly   clear

This page is intentionally left blank.

Task 1 Part D – Assessments

Daily Assessment Records

LESSON NUMBER:

QUESTION 1

Did the student participate when called upon?

QUESTION 2

Did the student participate in paired activity and/or group activity?

QUESTION 3

Did the student provide correct responses when called upon?

QUESTION 4

Did the student show learning toward the objective of the lesson?

QUESTION 5

What score did the student receive on worksheet? Document student's performance related to the worksheet.

Additional Comments:

QUESTION 1

Direction: Underline the noun in the sentence below.

The house was white with many windows.

QUESTION 2

Direction: Underline the noun in the sentence below.

Walking home, Jenny was really scared of the dogs she saw in the morning.

QUESTION 3

Direction: Underline **all** nouns in the sentence below.

Jack and Blair are going to the store next week to get backpacks.

QUESTION 4

Direction: Underline **all** nouns in the sentence below.

He wanted cars and videos for his birthday.

QUESTION 5

Direction: Write one sentence using the following two nouns:

watch   phone

QUESTION 6

Direction: Write one sentence using the following two nouns:

doctor   hat

QUESTION 7

Direction: Read the following short paragraph and underline all nouns.

Many cars exist in the world today. There are different color cars, and there are many different size cars. My uncle has a blue car, but he is looking to get a red car. He is planning to take me to the car dealership to look for cars next week. I am very excited about getting to go with my uncle.

QUESTION 8

Direction: Read the following short paragraph and underline all nouns.

Soccer is played throughout the world, and soccer is a fun sport to play. The basic concept to soccer is two teams playing with a round ball on a field. Each team attempts to put the ball in the other team's goal.

QUESTION 9

Explain the definition of a noun.

QUESTION 10

Circle all the words in the list below that can be a noun.

run – quick – help – car – cup – extreme – party – game – blue – homework – scary – cold

Lesson 2 – Worksheet – Pronouns

QUESTION 1

Direction: Underline the pronoun in the sentence below.

The house was white with many windows, so he was going to look to buy the house.

QUESTION 2

Direction: Underline the pronoun in the sentence below.

Walking home, Jenny was really scared of the dogs she saw in the morning.

QUESTION 3

Direction: Underline **all** pronouns in the sentence below.

He was not happy with the cup as it had a crack.

QUESTION 4

Direction: Underline **all** pronouns in the sentence below.

He wanted cars and videos for his birthday, but he was only allowed one present.

QUESTION 5

Direction: Write one sentence using the following two pronouns:

his   it

QUESTION 6

Direction: Write one sentence using the following two pronouns:

they   her

QUESTION 7

Direction: Read the following short paragraph and underline all pronouns.

Many cars exist in the world today. There are different color cars, and there are many different size cars. My uncle has a blue car, but he is looking to get a red car. He is planning to take me to the car dealership to look for cars next week. I am very excited about getting to go with my uncle.

QUESTION 8

Direction: Read the following short paragraph and underline all pronouns.

Soccer is played throughout the world, and soccer is a fun sport to play. The basic concept to soccer is two teams playing with a round ball on a field. Each team attempts to put the ball in the other team's goal.

QUESTION 9

Explain the definition of a pronoun.

QUESTION 10

Circle all the words in the list below that can be a pronoun.

I – quick – he – car – cup – extreme – they – game – blue – homework – my – cold

QUESTION 1

Direction: Underline the verb in the sentence below.

The house is white with many windows.

QUESTION 2

Direction: Underline the verb in the sentence below.

Walking home, Jenny was really scared of the dogs she saw in the morning.

QUESTION 3

Direction: Underline **all** verbs in the sentence below.

Jack and Blair are going to the store next week to get backpacks, and they might go to the movies too.

QUESTION 4

Direction: Underline **all** verbs in the sentence below.

He wanted cars and videos for his birthday, but his mother said he can only have one present.

QUESTION 5

Direction: Write one sentence using the following two verbs:

sleep   go

QUESTION 6

Direction: Write one sentence using the following two verbs:

eat   ran

QUESTION 7

Direction: Read the following short paragraph and underline all verbs.

Many cars exist in the world today. There are different color cars, and there are many different size cars. My uncle has a blue car, but he is looking to get a red car. He is planning to take me to the car dealership to look for cars next week. I am very excited about getting to go with my uncle.

QUESTION 8

Direction: Read the following short paragraph and underline all verbs.

Soccer is played throughout the world, and soccer is a fun sport to play. The basic concept to soccer is two teams playing with a round ball on a field. Each team attempts to put the ball in the other team's goal.

QUESTION 9

Explain the definition of a verb.

QUESTION 10

Circle all the words in the list below that can be a verb.

run – quick – help – car – cup – extreme – party – game – go – homework – scary – cold – ran - sleep

Lesson 4 – Worksheet – Adverbs

QUESTION 1

Direction: Underline the adverb in the sentence below.

Jimmy was speaking softly as he had a cold.

QUESTION 2

Direction: Underline the adverb in the sentence below.

He plays the piano very beautifully as he has had many years of practice.

QUESTION 3

Direction: Underline **all** adverbs in the sentence below.

Jane talked loudly in the hall, and he was talking quietly inside the room.

QUESTION 4

Direction: Underline **all** adverbs in the sentence below.

He ate the chocolate candy greedily and quickly, so he suddenly got sick.

QUESTION 5

Direction: Write one sentence using the following two adverbs:

badly   rapidly

QUESTION 6

Direction: Write one sentence using the following two adverbs:

sadly   warmly

QUESTION 7

Direction: Read the following short paragraph and underline all adverbs.

Many cars exist in the world today. There are different color cars, and there are many different size cars. My uncle has a blue car, but he is looking to get a red car. He is planning to take me to the car dealership to carefully look for cars next week. I am extremely excited about getting to go with my uncle.

QUESTION 8

Direction: Read the following short paragraph and underline all adverbs.

Soccer is played throughout the world, and soccer is a extremely fun sport to play. The basic concept to soccer is two teams diligently playing with a round ball on a field. Each team attempts to put the ball in the other team's goal.

QUESTION 9

Explain the definition of a adverb.

QUESTION 10

Circle all the words in the list below that can be a adverb.

run – quickly – help – car – cup – extreme – party – game – go – clumsily – scary –
coldly – ran - sleep

Lesson 5 – Worksheet

Part A – Adjectives

QUESTION 1

Direction: Underline the adjective in the sentence below.

The smell of the wild soil was strong.

QUESTION 2

Direction: Underline the adjective in the sentence below.

Suddenly, several cars came into the streets.

QUESTION 3

Direction: Underline **all** adjectives in the sentence below.

Jake had a red shirt, and Max had a blue shirt, which he got from Jake last year.

QUESTION 4

Direction: Underline **all** adjectives in the sentence below.

She had a black car, and she was not going to sell it for a smaller car.

QUESTION 5

Direction: Write one sentence using the following two adjectives:

big   green

QUESTION 6

Direction: Write one sentence using the following two adjectives:

little   large

QUESTION 7

Direction: Read the following short paragraph and underline all adjectives.

Many cars exist in the world today. There are different color cars, and there are many different size cars. My uncle has a blue car, but he is looking to get a red car. He is planning to take me to the car dealership to look for cars next week. I am very excited about getting to go with my uncle.

QUESTION 8

Direction: Read the following short paragraph and underline all adjectives.

Soccer is played throughout the world, and soccer is a fun sport to play. The basic concept to soccer is two teams playing with a round ball on a field. Each team attempts to put the ball in the other team's goal.

QUESTION 9

Explain the definition of an adjective.

QUESTION 10

Circle all the words in the list below that can be an adjective.

run – quick – help – is – day – extreme – party – game – blue – gentle – scary – cold

Part B – Adverbs

QUESTION 1

Direction: Underline the adverb in the sentence below.

You handwriting is neatly written.

QUESTION 2

Direction: Underline the adverb in the sentence below.

The snow fell steadily, and December had not even started.

QUESTION 3

Direction: Underline the adverb in the sentence below.

My brother drives very carefully as he has been in car accidents in the past.

Part C – Verbs

QUESTION 1

Direction: Underline the verb in the sentence below.

You handwriting is neatly written.

QUESTION 2

Direction: Underline the verb in the sentence below.

The snow fell steadily, and December had not even started.

QUESTION 3

Define verb.

Part D – Pronouns

QUESTION 1

Direction: Change the underline word/words to a pronoun.

Jake played outside with <u>Matt and Blake</u>.

QUESTION 2

Direction: Underline the pronoun in the sentence below.

Coming home from camp, he was not happy to his room empty.

QUESTION 3

Direction: Underline the pronoun in the sentence below.

I was not going to work with Jenny for my science project; Jenny is very mean.

Part E – Nouns

QUESTION 1

Direction: Underline the noun in the sentence below.

Last night, the sky was very cloudy, and rain poured all night due to the tropical storm.

QUESTION 2

Direction: Read the following short paragraph and underline all nouns.

Soccer is played throughout the world, and soccer is a fun sport to play. The basic concept to soccer is two teams playing with a round ball on a field. Each team attempts to put the ball in the other team's goal.

QUESTION 3

Define noun.

Task 1 Part E – Planning Commentary

QUESTION 1 – Alignment of the Learning Goal, Standard, Objectives, and Planned Support

Part A

Lesson	Lesson Objective	Planned Supports to Address Learning Goal
Learning Goal: The learning goal is for the focus learner to understand, recognize, and use pronouns, nouns, verbs, adjectives, and adverbs when reading and writing.		
Relevant Standard: CCSS.ELA-Literacy.L.3.1.a Explain the function of nouns, pronouns, verbs, adjectives, and adverbs in general and their functions in particular sentences.		
Lesson 1	The objective is for the students to read text and to complete worksheet related to understanding, identifying, and using nouns.	anchor chart, video, reading text, and repetition
Lesson 2	The objective is for the students to gain knowledge related to pronouns and to show competencies by completing a worksheet related to pronouns.	anchor chart, paired-activity, posters, and repetition
Lesson 3	The objective is for the students to gain knowledge related to verbs and to show competencies by completing a worksheet related to verbs.	anchor chart, video, reading text, and repetition
Lesson 4	The objective is for the students to gain knowledge related to adverbs and to show competencies by completing a worksheet related to adverbs.	anchor chart, paired-activity, and repetition
Lesson 5	The objective is for the students to gain knowledge related to adjectives and to show competencies by completing a worksheet related to adjectives.	anchor chart, video, paired-activity, and repetition

Part B

The selected learning goal is academic but is not aligned with an IEP goal. The following provides information on how the planned supports align with the learning goal.

Anchor Charts – In each lesson, anchor chart will be used to introduce the key part of speech (nouns, pronouns, verbs, adjectives, and adverbs). This is linked to the learning goal as the charts support the focus learner in understanding and recognizing nouns, pronouns, verbs, adjectives, and adverbs.

Repetition – Repetition is a strategy used to support the focus learner in understanding and maintaining knowledge. In each of the lessons, multiple activities will be undertaken to support the focus learner in understanding and applying knowledge related to the learning goal. For example, in lesson 1, the focus learner will be introduced to nouns via direct instruction with anchor charts. Then, the focus learner will repeat the definition of noun along with examples. Next, the focus learner will be shown a video related to nouns. The focus learner will practice identifying nouns when asked to for the sentence written on the Smart Board. Again, the focus learner will apply the knowledge of identifying noun when asked to find all nouns in an informational text. At the end of the lesson, the focus learner will complete a worksheet related to nouns.

Reading Text – When activities involved reading text, the text will be grade appropriate for the student to focus on identifying parts of speech. This prevented the focus learner from struggling to read and focus more on the learning goal.

Videos – When using videos, the content of the videos will be linked back to understanding and recognizing the parts of speech. This will support the student in applying the skill when reading and writing.

Paired Activities – Throughout the learning segment, the focus learner will be involved in paired activities, which will support the learning goal. The focus learner will be able to practice the skills in an environment that allowed him to make mistakes and obtain corrective feedback.

Posters – When using posters, the focus learner will be able to practice using the skill related to identifying parts of speech.

Part C

No additional special accommodations or modifications will be made in the learning environment instruction, or assessment.

134

Part D

The objectives of the lessons in the learning segment are purposely designed to support the focus learner to maximize gaining adequate knowledge related to the parts of speech. Each lesson objective focuses on only one part of speech; subsequently, this supports my focus learner in moving forward in achieving the learning goal and standard. By keeping the objective focused on only one part of speech, the focus learner will be able to engage in multiple activities to gain adequate knowledge. In addition, the focus learner will be adequately assessed in each lesson to ensure achievement for the objective. In the past, the focus learner has struggled to maintain knowledge when too much information is presented in one lesson. Breaking down one part of speech for each lesson supports how the focus learner has better acquired knowledge in the past.

Within each lesson, the learning tasks are sequenced to support the focus learner in gaining more independence in acquiring knowledge related to the objectives, standards, and learning goal. In each of the lesson, the teacher will introduce the concept of the lesson with anchor chart and discussion. Then, the focus learner will be involved in repeating the definition and providing examples, which gives the focus learner opportunity to show acquisition of new learning. Then, the student is shown either a video or posters with additional examples of the parts of speech. For example, in lessons 1, 3, and 5, a video will be shown related to noun, verb, and adjective, respectively. In lesson 2 and 4, posters will be shown with examples of pronoun and adverb, respectively. After that, the focus learner will be participating in learning tasks that are more engaging and challenging. In lesson 1 and 3, the focus learner will be involved in reading independently to identify parts of speech. In lesson 2, 4, and 5, the focus learner will participate in more involved activities such as writing sentences with parts of speech and identifying parts of speech. These activities link to the focus learner's prior knowledge as the student does know how to read and write at appropriate grade level. At the end of each lesson, the focus learner will be required to complete a worksheet independently.

All the materials and planned supports that will be used in the learning segment link back to the learning goal and standard. Visual aids, such as anchor charts and posters, directly will target on conveying to the focus learner knowledge related to the objective of the lesson. Since my focus learner has auditory processing disorder, in past learning, visual aids have supported him to learning. So, in teaching new learning, I strongly feel that these visual aids will support the student in accomplishing the learning goal. The videos used in the learning segment also link back to providing the focus learner with information about the parts of speech. For example, lesson 1 video will be about nouns, and lesson 3 video will be about verbs. Materials, such as reading text, are grade appropriate, which allow the student to focus on the learning goal instead of struggling to read. Another planned support that moved my focus learner to achieve the learning goal will be repetition. In past learning, the student has shown good competency achievement by repeating the tasks. In each lesson, the focus learner will be involved in multiple activities related to the objective of the lesson. In fact, in lesson 2, the student will be involved in working with nouns, which is linked back to lesson 1. In addition, in lesson 5, the focus learner's prior knowledge of nouns, pronouns, verbs, and adverbs are tested.

Question 2 – Knowledge of Focus Learner to Inform Teaching of the Learning Segment

Part A

The focus learner has the ability to write and read at a grade-appropriate level. The focus learner is not an avid reader, and he can improve on reading skills. In particular, the student is able to recall details from text, but he struggles with inferring. However, there is no impact to gaining knowledge in this learning segment. In regards to writing skills, the focus learner has written sentences in the past. In fact, the focus learner has written sentences unknowingly or knowingly with nouns, pronouns, verbs, adverbs, and adjectives. The focus learner has basic understanding of writing convection (spelling, capitalization, punctuation, and grammar). The focus learner has not had any formal lesson on any parts of speech, but has experience in using them in informal conversations.

The focus learner has used nouns, pronouns, verbs, adverbs, and adjectives verbally many times. However, the focus learner might have been unaware of what he was using. The focus learner was required to complete a pre-assessment related to the objectives of the lessons. The focus learner did not show any strong prior knowledge related to the parts of speech except for pronouns. The student got 3 out of 5 questions correct for the pre-assessment related to pronouns. In fact, for pre-assessment related to nouns and verbs, the student got one question correct. For adverbs, the student got all questions incorrect, and for adjectives, the student got two correct questions. From the baseline data, the focus learner showed lack of formal knowledge related to parts of speech.

Part B

My focus learner has mild form of autism, so he has some social interaction issues. The focus learner sometimes becomes rude or yells when he does not get what he wants. Aside from that, the focus learner is able to engage with other students. In fact, he has shown that he can work

136

with other students in the past, but time to time, he has issues interacting in a positive manner. In group activities, the student does sometime need support to get involved; he never takes any lead role in engagement when working in groups. The focus learner can establish short and long term relationships with peers. His impulse control is not the best, but it is not severely bad. As indicated, he gets very distraught when he does not get what he wants. My focus learner does have ADHD, and he is not able to stay focused for lengthy period of time. The student is aware that he has issues staying focused as it is indicated in his IEP.

Part C

The focus learner is interested in playing outside more than focusing on core academic studies. In addition, the focus learner is very interested in cars as he has a backpack with a car logo, and he wears clothing with car logos. Moreover, the focus learner is very interested in drawing. In fact, his drawing abilities are above average. Even though the focus learner lacks interest in core academics, he is able to acquire knowledge when provided with the right supports, which is a strength of his. Besides yelling and being rude when he does not get what he wants, the focus learner is able to engage with others in learning, which is a strength of his. Another strength of the student is being able to learn better when using visual aids, which might be linked to the fact that he has auditory processing disorder; visual aids support him during learning.

The focus learner's family came to the United States from Mexico. He speaks fluent Spanish, and he has learned English better than other English language learners. This is primary due to the fact he started his education in the United States from kindergarten. In past learning, the student has discussed what his family has done on Cinco de Mayo. Also, the student brings lunch from home, and his mother does cook traditional meals for him. The focus learner has a connection to his roots from Mexico.

The focus learner's parents both work. His father is a full-time truck driver while his mother is a part-time clerk at an insurance company. He does not come from a rich family. In fact, with having 5 siblings, he comes from a low-income family. The focus learner is the only sibling with learning disabilities. He is the youngest of the 5 siblings, so he does get support from his brothers and sisters. His siblings support him in doing his homework. All of his siblings live in the same house, so the family is close-knit.

The school is located in the center of a culturally diverse community. The focus learner does not live in a gated community. In fact, the focus learner resides in a poor community. The neighborhoods and school includes a very large, well established Hispanic-black population with enrollment of Latino and Hispanic being 45% and blacks being 50%. The rest of the population is whites or Asian Pacific Islanders. Since the focus learner reside in a poor community, there are free resources provided by third party organizations such as health fairs, free lunch programs during summer, after school tutoring, and reading programs.

Part D

Not applicable

Question 3 – Supporting Learning

Part A

The following explains how learning tasks, materials, and planned supports address the focus learner's needs, strengths and interests.

Videos – The videos that will be used in the learning segmented supported my focus learner's need as he has auditory processing disorder. Having images and audio re-informing the student about the parts of speech will play a critical role in the focus learner achieving the learning goal.

Visual Aids (Posters and Anchor Charts) – With my focus learning having auditory processing disorder, visual aids will support him in the learning process. Each of the parts of speech is introduced with anchor charts. The focus learner is ESL, so the anchor chart supports his language needs.

Reading Text – In lesson 1 and 3, I will include reading text to find parts of speech. The reading texts selected are linked to the focus learner's interest in sports.

Engaging In-Class Paired/Group Activities – Throughout the learning segment, I included paired activities and group activities to target both needs and strengths of the focus student. The student has shown the ability to work in group setting, but still needs to practice being respectful. As a result, prior to engaging in any group/paired activities, the focus learner will be informed to be respectful to peers. In lesson 2, I had the focus learner work with index cards in paired activity to identify nouns or pronouns. In lessons 4 and 5, the focus learner will write a sentence on index card and exchange with peers to determine parts of speech. In lesson 5, the focus learner is involved in a group activity in placing the sticky note in the correct section on a poster. Engaging activities are also linked to my focus learner's need of staying focused. My focus learner has ADHD and can lose focus quickly. Having engaging activities will support the learner in staying alert. Moreover, the focus learner does have mild autism, so having the focus learner engaged with students can support him in better interacting with peers.

Part B

The following are ways the focus learner will be challenged during the learning segment:

In-Class Discussion – In each lesson, I will put sentences on the Smart Board, and I will have the students identify the parts of speech. In addition, the students will discuss if the answers are correct or incorrect. By getting the focus learner involved in informing if answers are correct or incorrect, the learner will be further challenged. Moreover, in some sentences, I will include multiple parts of speeches, which will further challenge the focus learner to look deeper.

Reading Text – Having the focus learner find the parts of speech in reading text provides challenge to the learner as he is forced to apply skills in a different setting.

Visual Aids (Anchor Charts and Poster) – When using poster, there are example sentences on the front and on the back are the answers. The focus learner is challenged to find the part of speech in the sentences when working with posters.

Engaging In-Class Paired/Group Activities – The focus learner will be challenged a lot during paired activities and group activities as the student will be undertaking different activities. For example, in lesson 4 and 5, the focus learner will be required to come up with the sentence using parts of speech properly. Then, the focus learner will be paired with another student to exchange index cards and determine the parts of speech.

Part C

The following provides justification for selecting the learning tasks, materials, and planned supports:

Videos – My focus learner is a visual learner, so using videos is a good way to target his strength. Moreover, this is linked to Kishore visual learning theory in which the visual aids help in collaboration and improvement in the cognitive sense and the learning process. In particular, the visual aids can assist the teacher to improve appearance in the class than the traditional ways of learning. In addition, the focus learner is an ESL student, so using videos support his language needs.

Visual Aids (Anchor Charts and Poster) – The focus learner has auditory processing disorder, which impacts processing of what is heard. Using anchor charts and posters supported the focus learner's needs. The anchor charts are displayed during instruction for the focus learner to refer back too.

Repetition – This was another planned support that was used that will support my focus learner's behavior. My learner has autism, and he sometime repeats his behavior. To design lessons that included repetition of acquiring knowledge supports his behavior. In addition, since my learner has auditory processing disorder, repetition allows the learner to gain knowledge in different modes. Designing lessons with the repetition of activities is linked to multiple-trace theory, which indicates that repetition improves learning because finding at least one trace of an event becomes easier when there are more traces of that event in memory.

Engaging In-Class Paired/Group Activities – Throughout the learning segment, I included paired activities and group activities to target both needs and strengths of the focus student. The student has shown the ability to work in group setting, but still needs to practice being respectful. In addition, including engaging activities is linked to Lev Vygotsky concept of social constructivism, in which social interaction with others assists the learner in putting meaning to information. Vygotsky noted a Zone of Proximal Development, in which learners can develop a certain level of meaning on their own but can grow even greater after interacting with classmates and instructors.

Part D

Lesson 1

The students will acquire knowledge related to noun via direct instruction, video, and in-class activities. The students will be able to generalize the knowledge by identifying nouns in sentences and reading texts.

To maintain skill, the students will practice identifying nouns in multiple ways:

- identifying nouns in sentences written on Smart Board
- reading short informational text and identifying nouns
- completing worksheet identifying nouns

The students will be involved in grading themselves after reading the short informational text and identifying nouns. During in-class activities, if the student is incorrect, he or she will have the opportunity to try again to reach the correct answer.

Lesson 2

The students will acquire knowledge related to pronouns. The students will be using this knowledge and skill in different environments (paired activity and independent activity). Also, I will include some sentences that have multiple pronouns for students to find, allowing them to generalize the knowledge acquired.

To maintain skill, the students will practice identifying pronouns in multiple ways:

- identifying pronoun(s) in sentences displayed on posters
- identifying and using pronouns during in-class activity
- completing worksheet identifying pronouns

The students will be involved in grading themselves after completing worksheet related to pronouns. During in-class activities, if the student is incorrect, he or she will have the opportunity to try again to reach the correct answer.

Lesson 3

The students will acquire knowledge related to verb. The students will be using this knowledge and skill in different environments (group activity and independent activity). The students will be able to generalize knowledge when they encounter sentences with more than one verb.

To maintain skill, the students will practice identifying verbs in multiple ways:

- identifying verbs in sentence displayed in the video
- reading short informational text and identifying verbs
- completing worksheet identifying verbs

The students will be involved in grading themselves after reading the short informational text and identifying verbs. During in-class activities, if the student is incorrect, he or she will have the opportunity to try again to reach the correct answer.

Lesson 4

The students will acquire knowledge related to adverbs and examples of adverbs. The students will be using this knowledge and skill in different environments (paired activity and independent activity).

To maintain skill, the students will practice identifying adverbs in multiple ways:

- identifying adverbs in sentences displayed on posters
- identifying and using adverbs during paired activity
- completing worksheet identifying adverbs

The students will be involved in grading themselves after completing worksheet related to adverbs. During in-class activities, if the student is incorrect, he or she will have the opportunity to try again to reach the correct answer.

Lesson 5

The students will acquire knowledge related to adjectives and examples of adjectives. The students will be using this knowledge and skill in different environments (paired activity and independent activity).

To maintain skill, the students will practice identifying adjectives in multiple ways:

- identifying adjectives in sentence displayed on poster
- identifying and using adjectives during flashcard activity
- completing worksheet identifying adjectives

During in-class activities, if the student is incorrect, he or she will have opportunity to try again to reach the correct answer. I will also have the focus learner review poster with sticky notes to see if there are any mistakes that need to be corrected.

Question 4 – Supporting the Focus Learner's Use of Expressive/Receptive Communication

Part A

The communication skill the focus learner will need to use to participate and to demonstrate learning is selecting the correct parts of speech.

Part B

In lesson 1, I will use anchor chart to introduce noun. In addition, I will use a video to re-teach noun. These supports will allow the focus learner to acquire knowledge related to noun. In addition, I will have the focus learner read a short information text and require him to select all the nouns used. This will support the focus learner to generalize the knowledge acquired related to identifying nouns.

In lesson 2, step 3, I will use an anchor chart to introduce pronoun, and in step 5, I will use posters to allow focus learner to use communication skill of selecting pronoun in sentences. Moreover, I will do an in-class activity where I have the focus learner select the pronoun in sentence written on the Smart Board. Another support that will be used in this lesson is group activity where students write a sentence on the selected part of speech along with identifying the part of speech (Step 7). In this lesson, repetition of activities will allow the focus learner to maintain the communication skill of selecting pronouns.

In lesson 3, an anchor chart (Step 3) and a video (Step 5) will be used to help the student acquire knowledge to be able to use communication skill of selecting verbs. In step 6, I will include some sentences with two verbs to identify, which allow the students to generalize the skill of selecting verbs. In addition, I will have the focus learner read a short informational text and require him to select all the nouns used. This will support the focus learner to generalize the knowledge acquired related to identifying verbs.

In lesson 4, step 3, I will use anchor chart to introduce adverb, and in step 5, I will use posters to allow focus learner to use communication skill of selecting adverb in sentences. Another support that will be used in this lesson is paired activity where students write sentences with adverb on index cards, exchange cards with partner, and identify the adverb (Step 7 and 8). In this lesson, repetition of activities will allow the focus learner to maintain the communication skill of selecting adverb.

In lesson 5, anchor chart (Step 3) and video (Step 5) will be used to help the student acquire knowledge to be able to use communication skill of selecting adjectives. In Step 6, I will include some sentences with two adjectives to identify, which allow the students to generalize the skill of selecting adjectives. Another support that will be used in this lesson is paired activity where students write sentences using adjective on index cards, exchange cards with partner, and identify the adjective (Step 7 and 8).

Question 5 – Monitoring Learning

Part A

The baseline data included a worksheet with five parts: nouns, pronouns, verbs, adverbs, and adjectives. There were 5 questions for each part. The baseline data allowed me to gain understanding of focus learner's knowledge related to the learning goal.

In each of the lessons, I included a formal assessment related to the objective of the lesson. So I will be able to see the knowledge the focus learner obtained for nouns, pronouns, verbs, adverbs, and adjectives. In each assessment, to challenge the focus learner, he will be required to write sentences using the parts of speech, identify parts of speech in sentences, and/or identify parts of speech in short reading text. The performance of the focus learner on the assessments will allow me to see how he is progressing related to the objective of each lesson. To support my focus learner, the assessment will be timed, but ample time will be given to the student. In addition, once the student is completed, I will have the student go back and check his work.

The daily assessment records will require documenting the following related to the focus learner:

- Did the student participate when called upon?
- Did the student provide correct responses when asked questions?
- Did the student participate in independent, paired, and/or group activities?
- What score did the student receive on the lesson worksheet?

Observing the level of engagement, documenting incorrect responses, and grading the student's worksheet will provide evidence of the student progressing toward the lesson objectives and learning goal.

Part B

Throughout the learning segment, the focus learner is involved in monitoring his learning. In lesson 1 and 3, after underlining the parts of speech in the reading text, the focus learner will be given a red pen to self check. In lesson 2 and 4, the focus learner grade will be involved in grading his own worksheet with a red pen. In lesson 5, after placing the sticky notes on the poster, the focus learner will have a chance to correct any errors he sees on the poster. Taking these steps allows the focus learner to be engaged in monitoring progress.

Task 2: Part A – Video Clips

The video summary is provided below for this Special Education edTPA® assessment portfolio:

- Instruction was done with 6 students.

- Instruction took place in a regular classroom.

- Students were sitting around a circle table.

- Clip 1 includes Lesson 4 from Step 3 to Step 7. The complete Step 7 is not shown. The clip ends shortly after the student complete exchanging the index cards. The clip is around 12 minutes. See lesson plans for the steps.

- Clip 2 includes Lesson 5, and the clip shows only Step 8 and Step 9. The clip is around 8 minutes. See lesson plans for the steps.

This page is intentionally left blank.

Task 2: Part B – Instruction Commentary

Question 1

Clip 1 shows lesson plan 4. Clip 2 shows lesson plan 5. No additional changes were made to the lesson plans.

Question 2

Part A – Not applicable

Part B – The focus learner is the one in the red shirt.

Question 3 – Promoting a Positive Learning Environment

Part A

The following are ways respect for and rapport was provided to all learners:

- The students were told to raise their hands if they wanted to speak, so everyone can be heard. In fact, throughout the clips, students raise their hands to speak (Clip 1: timestamp: 2:15 and 3:25).

- Instead of pointing to the students, I call them by their first name, which is an indication that I see them as individuals (Clip 1: timestamp: 1:15 and 2:30).

- I made sure to use a positive tone throughout the learning segment to keep students engaged in the learning along with fostering a safe learning environment (Clip 1 and 2: shown throughout the clips). Moreover, when students were distracted, I redirected the students in a respectful manner to complete the activities (Clip 1: timestamp: 10:15).

- My focus learner has auditory processing disorder, so I made sure to provide appropriate response time to support him. This was done multiple times during the learning segment. For example, when I asked the student to identify the adverb in the sentence written on the Smart Board, I allowed the student to think for about 1 minute (Clip 1: timestamp: 6:15).

- Another way I showed rapport for all learners is by giving all students opportunity to respond and participate. For example, I tried to make sure to call on different students (Clip 1: timestamp: 5:00-10:00).

- Another way I showed rapport is by making connection to students' interest and hobbies. For example, when I wrote sentences on the Smart Board, I made sure to write about cars and sports as those are interests my focus learner has along with his peers (Clip 1: timestamp: 6:15).

- When introducing the definition of adverb, I was very positive and enthusiastic about teaching this to students (Clip 1: timestamp: 0:56). This showed the students that I was passionate about teaching, hoping to brush that off to the focus learner.

Part B

The following were undertaken to provide a positive learning environment that supported and challenged the focus learner:

- When the focus learner was incorrect, I did not provide the correct answers. Instead, I provided hints to allow the focus learner to independently arrive at the right answer. When the student was incorrect in identifying the adverb, I told the student "that is a noun." The student then independently found the adverb (Clip 1: timestamp: 6:15). Taking this approach also challenged the focus learner to think deeper.

- Throughout the learning segment, I provided positive feedback to the focus student. For example, when the focus learner was working in paired activity, I said "Excellent work; you are doing just better and better" (Clip 1: timestamp: 11:15). I also provided positive feedback when the focus learner was working in paired activity related to adjectives (Clip 2: timestamp: 2:25).

- Another way a positive learning environment was established was using a scaffolding approach to teaching adverbs. I used anchor charts to show the meaning of adverb (Clip 1: timestamp: 0:55). Then, I had the focus learner repeat the definition along with examples (Clip 1: timestamp: 2:15). Then, I had an activity for adverbs with support from peers. When the student gradually work more independently, the chances of success are higher, which is shown when the focus learner is working in paired activity (Clip 1:

timestamp: 10:00 and Clip 2: timestamp: 0:00 – 4:00). A positive environment is established when the focus learner is set to succeed.

- I also included paired activities throughout the learning segment to support the focus learner in acquiring knowledge related to the learning goal (Clip 1: timestamp: 10:00 and Clip 2: timestamp: 0:00 – 4:00). Working with peers is a support system in the learning process.

- I challenged the focus learner by having him apply the knowledge of identifying adverbs and adjectives in different activities, such as index card activity (Clip 1: timestamp: 10:15) and poster activity (Clip 2: timestamp: 9:12).

- The anchor chart were used to support my student as my student has auditory processing disorder, so having visuals will support him in learning process (Clip 1: timestamp: 0:15). Accommodating the focus learner's learning disabilities and language needs was a way of establishing a positive learning environment.

Question 4 – Engaging and Motivating the Focus Learner

Part A

A scaffolding approach was used to engage and motivate the focus learner to acquire and apply knowledge related to the learning goal. In lesson 4, adverb was introduced with an anchor chart along with examples. Then, the focus learner was involved in reiterating the meaning of adverb (Clip 1: timestamp: 2:15). Afterward, the focus learner was involved in identifying adverb with support from the teacher and peers. By taking a scaffolding approach, the focus learner was not only engaged, but also learning the skills to become more independent.

I also related to focus learner's interest when using sentences on Smart Board, which was a way to motivate the learner. For example, sentences used were related to cars, sports, and drawings. My focus learner has ADHD, so this approach worked well to keep the student motivated.

Having the focus learner work in pairs and group setting engaged the learner to be more involved (Clip 1: timestamp: 10:15 and Clip 2: timestamp: 0:00-4:00). As indicated, my student has ADHD, so he can lose focus quickly. However, when working with peers, the focus learner does not lose attention.

I also made sure the content and questions were at the right level of my focus learner. I did not want to put my focus learner in a struggling position to learn due to the lessons being outside of his current capabilities.

Another way that engaged the focus learner is by using different materials such as index cards, posters, anchor charts, and sticky notes (Clip 1 and Clip 2). This prevented the focus learner from becoming bored.

Part B

Since the focus learner is able to read and write at appropriate level, I included activities that involved the focus learner to write. For example, the focus learner had to write sentence using adverbs and adjectives (Clip 1: timestamp: 11:55 and Clip 2: timestamp: 0:15). Since the focus learner has unknowingly used nouns, pronouns, verbs, adverbs, and adjectives, this learning segment is linked to knowledge the focus learner has been exposed too. Since my focus learner has ADHD, I included paired and group activities in my instruction to keep the student focused and alert (Clip 1: timestamp: 10:00 and Clip 1: timestamp 0:00 – 4:00). Since the focus learner has 5 siblings, the focus learner has experience working and engaging with others. I also took into account personal asset by incorporating examples that link to focus learner's interest. For example, I included sentences about cars and sports, as my learner has great interest in these things. The focus learner comes from Mexico and is an English language learner, so I included language supports such as anchor charts in instruction to help the focus learner acquire knowledge.

Part C

The focus learner was involved in multiple activities involving adverbs, which supported him in maintaining knowledge and skill of identifying adverbs. The focus learner identified adverb in sentences placed on Smart Board along with identifying adverbs in paired activity (Clip 1: timestamp: 6:15). Similarly, for adjectives, I had the focus learner involved in multiple activities, such as paired activity and poster activity, which also kept the focus learner engaged.

Giving the focus learner a second attempt to correct himself allowed him to independently arrive at the correct answer. When the student was incorrect in identifying the adverb, I told the student "that is a noun" (Clip 1: timestamp: 6:15). The student then independently found the adverb. Also, in lesson 5, after everyone placed their sticky notes on the poster, I gave the focus

150

learner opportunity to review to see if he saw any mistakes that need to be corrected (Clip 2: timestamp: 7:10).

Giving direct instruction via anchor charts and using a scaffolding approach allowed the focus learner to become more independent in learning tasks. In lesson 4 paired activity, the focus learner did not need any direction or support to complete; the student was active in completing the activity (Clip 1: timestamp: 10:00 – 12:00).

Question 5 – Deepening Learning

Part A

I directly asked the focus learner questions to elicit responses. For example, I asked the focus learner to provide me the definition of adverb. I immediately responded to the focus learner by saying "Good job" (Clip 1: timestamp: 2:15). I also got the student involved in in-class activity by having him identify adverb in sentences. When the student was incorrect in identifying the adverb, I told the student "that is a noun" (Clip 1: timestamp: 6:15). Getting the focus learner involved in activities with peers was another way I elicit responses. For example, in lesson 5, the focus learner had to write sentence using adjectives (Clip 2: timestamp: 0:15). Moreover, I provided positive feedback throughout the learning segment to keep the student engaged. Keeping a positive environment made the focus learner more inclined to provide responses.

Part B

In lesson 4, I had the student identify the adverb in the sentences written on the Smart Board. However, the student was incorrect, so I provided feedback saying "that is a noun" (Clip 1: timestamp: 6:15). The student was able to use that feedback to arrive at the correct answer. Communicating to the student that he was correct allowed the focus learner to continue to get questions correct in paired activity (Clip 1: timestamp: 10:00-12:00 and Clip 2: timestamp: 0:00 – 4:00). The focus learner was also given opportunity to apply feedback during poster activity. When the focus learner was asked to review the poster and to fix any mistakes, opportunity was given to apply feedback given in the previous lessons (Clip 2: timestamp: 7:10).

Part C

The following shows my action to get the focus learner to self-evaluate and self-correct to improve performance:

- In each lesson, I had the focus learner complete a worksheet. Once completed, I gave the focus learner a red pen for self-grading purposes. I went over each question and had the focus learner correct himself on his paper.

- Instead of giving the correct answer when the student was wrong, I provided a second chance to get the student to correct himself. For example, in lesson 4, I had the student identify the adverb in the sentence written on the Smart Board. However, the student was incorrect, so I provided feedback saying "that is a noun" (Clip 1: timestamp: 6:15). The student was able to use that feedback to arrive at the correct answer.

- In lesson 5, when working in paired activity, the focus learner was incorrect in identifying the adjective, so I said "Are you sure?" This gave the focus learner another chance to self-correct himself (Clip 2: timestamp: 2:35).

- The focus learner was given another opportunity to correct mistakes during activity involving poster and sticky notes. I asked the focus learner to look at the poster and correct any mistakes that he saw before I went over the correct answers (Clip 2: timestamp: 7:15).

Question 6 – Supporting Teaching and Learning

Part A

The following explains how materials, planned supports, and instructional strategies allowed the focus learner to progress toward the objectives:

Anchor Charts – With my focus learner having auditory processing disorder, visual aids help my focus learner progress toward the objectives. For example, in lesson 4, I used anchor chart to introduce adverbs, which was critical for the student in learning about adverbs (Clip 1: timestamp: 0:50).

Index Card - Another material used was index cards for the focus learner to write sentences using parts of speech; this engaged the learner to show learning related to the objectives (Clip 1: timestamp: 10:00-12:00 and Clip 2: timestamp: 0:00-4:00).

Posters - In lesson 4, I also used posters to show example sentences of adverbs and engaged the focus learner to identify the adverbs (Clip 1: timestamp: 3:25). The sentences used on these posters were age appropriate.

Engaging In-Class Paired/Group Activities – Throughout the learning segment, I included paired activities and group activities as these were age appropriate activities but also linked to focus learner's strength of working with others. In lessons 4 and 5, the focus learner wrote a sentence on index card and exchange with peers to determine parts of speech (Clip 1: timestamp: 10:00-12:00 and Clip 2: timestamp: 0:00-4:00). In lesson 5, the focus learner is involved in a group activity in placing the sticky note in the correct section on a poster (Clip 2: timestamp: 4:00-4:00). Engaging activities also linked to my focus learner's need of staying focused. My focus learner has ADHD and can lose focus quickly. Having engaging activities supported the learner in staying alert. Moreover, the focus learner does have mild form of autism, so having the focus learner engage with students can support him in better interacting with peers.

Repetition – This strategy supported my focus learner as he has auditory processing disorder, so having him do multiple activities on the same objective will be valuable. The focus learner was involved in identifying adverb on poster, Smart Board, and paired activity (Clip 1: timestamp: 3:15, 6:15, 10:00-12:00).

Part B

Giving the focus learner a second chance to obtain correct answer is linked to self-directed learning strategy. When the student was asked to identify the adverb for the sentence on the poster board, I said "Double check your work." This engaged the focus learner to think again to reach the correct answer (Clip 1: timestamp: 3:15). When having the focus learner write sentences on index cards for his peers to find the part of speech, the focus learner was involved in the developing a self-directed learning strategy (Clip 1: timestamp: 10:00-12:00 and Clip 2: timestamp: 0:00-4:00). After the students were finished placing the sticky note in the correct section on poster, I asked the focus learner to correct any mistake, which was engaging the student in self-directed learning strategy (Clip 1: timestamp: 7:15). Scaffolding was another strategy use to allow my focus learner to become more confidence in using self-directed learning. Having the student learn adverbs with direct instruction, in-class discussion, and paired activity allow the student to become proficient in identifying adverbs. As a result, when he saw a sticky note not belonging in the adverb section, he was able to correct the mistake (Clip 2: timestamp: 7:15).

Question 7 – Analyzing Teaching

Part A

The following are changes I recommend to better support or extend the student's performance:

- I included posters with just sentences with no images. The change I would make is including images in the poster and anchor charts.

- When students were working in paired activity, the feedback I provided was mostly general, such as "Good job" or "Excellent" (Clip 1: timestamp: 10:25 and Clip 2: timestamp: 3:15). I would have provided more detail feedback.

- When I had the student identify adverbs for sentences displayed on the poster, it is very clear I moved very quickly. The change would be to give more time for the student to respond.

- Include a different activity, such as a jeopardy game, as I used index card activity multiple times throughout the learning segment.

Part B

The following are reasons why the recommended changes would improve students' learning:

- Visual aids support my learner in acquiring knowledge, but also keep the student engaged. Moreover, Kishore visual learning theory states that visual aids help in collaboration and improvement in the cognitive sense and the learning process. Effective visual aids can support the focus learner to maintain information better.

- Research has shown that feedback is a tool to support students in improving learning as students figure out what they are doing right and wrong. Giving information to students regarding details of what he is doing incorrect can support him better in learning (Jake J., and Blair R. – Feedback Development).

- Giving additional time is supported by Mary Budd Rowe, an educational researcher. Giving the student longer response time help the student verbalize the response. The teacher is able to use the response to have a better and in-depth discussion.

- Including jeopardy game, or any other different activity, is related to differentiating instruction, which is linked to the research by Carol Ann Tomlinson. She emphasized that differentiation is tailoring instruction to meet individual needs. Differentiation is a way for teacher to respond to students' learning needs. In this case, using a different activity can help the focus learner generalize the knowledge in a different setting.

This page is intentionally left blank.

Task 3: Part A – Work Sample

Lesson 5 – Worksheet

Part A - Adjectives

QUESTION 1

Direction: Underline the adjective in the sentence below.

The smell of the wild soil was strong.

QUESTION 2

Direction: Underline the adjective in the sentence below.

Suddenly, several cars came into the streets.

QUESTION 3

Direction: Underline **all** adjectives in the sentence below.

Jake had a red shirt, and Max had a blue shirt, which he got from Jake last year.

QUESTION 4

Direction: Underline **all** adjectives in the sentence below.

She had a black car, and she was not going to sell it for a smaller car.

QUESTION 5

Direction: Write one sentence using the following two adjectives:

big   green

The big boy has a green shirt.

QUESTION 6

Direction: Write one sentence using the following two adjectives:

little   large

The little girl has a large cup.

QUESTION 7

Direction: Read the following short paragraph and underline all adjectives.

Many cars exist in the world today. There are different color cars, and there are many different size cars. My uncle has a blue car, but he is looking to get a red car. He is planning to take me to the car dealership to look for cars next week. I am very excited about getting to go with my uncle.

QUESTION 8

Direction Read the following short paragraph and underline all adjectives.

Soccer is played throughout the world, and soccer is a fun sport to play. The basic concept to soccer is two teams playing with a round ball on a field. Each team attempts to put the ball in the other team's goal.

QUESTION 9

Explain the definition of an adjective.

descibe noun

QUESTION 10

Circle all the words in the list below that can be an adjective.

run – quick – help – is – day – extreme – party – game – blue – gentle – scary – cold

Part B – Adverbs

QUESTION 1

Direction: Underline the adverb in the sentence below.

You handwriting is <u>neatly</u> written.

QUESTION 2

Direction: Underline the adverb in the sentence below.

The snow fell steadily, and December had not even started.

QUESTION 3

Direction: Underline the adverb in the sentence below.

My brother drives very <u>carefully</u> as he has been in car accidents in the past.

Part C - Verbs

QUESTION 1

Direction: Underline the verb in the sentence below.

You handwriting is neatly written.

QUESTION 2

Direction: Underline the verb in the sentence below.

The snow fell steadily, and December had not even started.

QUESTION 3

Define verb.

action

Part D – Pronouns

QUESTION 1

Direction: Change the underline word/words to a pronoun.

Jake played outside with <u>Matt and Blake</u>.

them

QUESTION 2

Direction Underline the pronoun in the sentence below.

Coming home from camp, he was not happy to his room empty.

QUESTION 3

Direction Underline the pronoun in the sentence below.

I was not going to work with Jenny for my science project; Jenny is very mean.

Part E – Nouns

QUESTION 1

Direction: Underline the noun in the sentence below.

Last night, the sky was very cloudy, and rain poured all night due to the tropical storm.

QUESTION 2

Direction Read the following short paragraph and underline all nouns.

Soccer is played throughout the world, and soccer is a fun sport to play. The basic concept to soccer is two teams playing with a round ball on a field. Each team attempts to put the ball in the other team's goal.

QUESTION 3

Define noun.

person place
thing

This page is intentionally left blank.

Task 3: Part B – Completed Daily Assessment Records and Baseline Data

Daily Assessment Records

LESSON NUMBER: 1

QUESTION 1

Did the student participate when called upon?

Yes

QUESTION 2

Did the student participate in paired activity and/or group activity?

Yes, some support provided

QUESTION 3

Did the student provide correct responses when called upon?

Yes

QUESTION 4

Did the student show learning toward the objective of the lesson?

Yes

QUESTION 5

What score did the student receive on the worksheet? Document student's performance related to the worksheet. 80% , only 2 incorrect

Additional Comments: Well done overall

Daily Assessment Records

LESSON NUMBER: 2

QUESTION 1

Did the student participate when called upon?

yes

QUESTION 2

Did the student participate in paired activity and/or group activity?

yes.

QUESTION 3

Did the student provide correct responses when called upon?

yes

QUESTION 4

Did the student show learning toward the objective of the lesson?

yes

QUESTION 5

What score did the student receive on worksheet? Document student's performance related to the worksheet.

100%

Additional Comments:

Very good Job :-)

Daily Assessment Records

LESSON NUMBER: 3

QUESTION 1

Did the student participate when called upon?

Yes

QUESTION 2

Did the student participate in paired activity and/or group activity?

Yes

QUESTION 3

Did the student provide correct responses when called upon?

Most of the time. Two responses incorrect

QUESTION 4

Did the student show learning toward the objective of the lesson?

Yes

QUESTION 5

What score did the student receive on the worksheet? Document student's performance related to the worksheet. 60%, need some improvement

Additional Comments: Need improvent on worksheet, but overall no major gaps.

Daily Assessment Records

LESSON NUMBER: 4

QUESTION 1

Did the student participate when called upon?

yes

QUESTION 2

Did the student participate in paired activity and/or group activity?

yes

QUESTION 3

Did the student provide correct responses when called upon?

yes, support was provided

QUESTION 4

Did the student show learning toward the objective of the lesson?

yes

QUESTION 5

What score did the student receive on the worksheet? Document student's
performance related to the worksheet. 70%

Additional Comments: Overall engagment was good
Super Job

Daily Assessment Records

LESSON NUMBER: 5

QUESTION 1

Did the student participate when called upon?

Yes

QUESTION 2

Did the student participate in paired activity and/or group activity?

Yes

QUESTION 3

Did the student provide correct responses when called upon?

Yes

QUESTION 4

Did the student show learning toward the objective of the lesson?

Yes

QUESTION 5

What score did the student receive on the worksheet? Document student's performance related to the worksheet. 82%

Additional Comments: Very Good Job overall.

Baseline Data Assignment

Part A – Nouns

Direction: Underline **all** the nouns in the following sentences.

Question 1

In the house, there was a big television.

Question 2

Jake is going to his brother's house for Thanksgiving.

Question 3

Your cat is tall.

Question 4

I want to eat in my room this weekend.

Question 5

The notebook was in the back of the room.

Part B – Pronouns

Direction: Underline **all** the pronouns in the following sentences.

Question 1

Juan quickly decided he was going to eat cupcakes.

Question 3

I was going to my friend's birthday party.

Question 2

They are going to the field trip next week.

Question 3

Your cat is tall.

Question 4

He is going to write on the wall with the makers.

Question 5

We are going on vacation to celebrate Christmas.

Part C – Verbs

Direction: Underline **all** the verbs in the following sentences.

Question 1

This baby cries all the time.

Question 2

Juan wrote his name on the top of the paper.

Question 3

Help is on the way.

Question 4

I am the leader.

Question 5

Jenny ran to get the mail.

Part D – Adverbs

Direction: Underline **all** the adverbs in the following sentences.

Question 1

This baby loudly cried during the night.

Question 2

Marty is regularly practicing throwing a ball.

Question 3

Help is quickly on the way.

Question 4

James checked his answers carefully before sending the worksheet to his teacher.

Question 5

Jenny slowly walked to get the mail.

Part E – Adjectives

Direction: Underline **all** the adjectives in the following sentences.

Question 1

John had a green backpack.

Question 2

His sister was very sad.

Question 3

Marty is slow in her reading.

Question 4

Mark is going to his mother's old house.

Question 5

Today, we are going to the highest mountain for fun.

Task 3: Part C – Evidence of Feedback

Lesson 5 – Worksheet

4 incorrect

Part A – Adjectives

(82%)

✓ QUESTION 1

Direction: Underline the adjective in the sentence below.

The <u>smell</u> of the wild soil was strong.

✓ QUESTION 2

Direction: Underline the adjective in the sentence below.

Suddenly, <u>several</u> cars came into the streets.

✓ QUESTION 3

Direction: Underline **all** adjectives in the sentence below.

Jake had a <u>red</u> shirt, and Max had a <u>blue</u> shirt, which he got from Jake <u>last</u> year.

✓ QUESTION 4

Direction: Underline **all** adjectives in the sentence below.

She had a <u>black</u> car, and she was not going to sell it for a <u>smaller</u> car.

Excellent Job

QUESTION 5

Direction: Write one sentence using the following two adjectives:

big   green

Good Job

The big boy has a green shirt.

QUESTION 6

Direction: Write one sentence using the following two adjectives:

little   large

The little girl has a large cup.

QUESTION 7

Direction: Read the following short paragraph and underline all adjectives.

Many cars exist in the world today. There are different color cars, and there are many different size cars. My uncle has a blue car, but he is looking to get a red car. He is planning to take me to the car dealership to look for cars next week. I am very excited about getting to go with my uncle.

QUESTION 8

Direction: Read the following short paragraph and underline all adjectives.

Soccer is played throughout the world, and soccer is a fun sport to play. The basic concept to soccer is two teams playing with a round ball on a field. Each team attempts to put the ball in the other team's goal.

not an adjective

QUESTION 9

Explain the definition of an adjective.

desube noun

QUESTION 10

Circle all the words in the list below that can be an adjective.

run – quick – help – is – day – extreme – party – game – blue – gentle – scary – cold

Part B – Adverbs

QUESTION 1

Direction: Underline the adverb in the sentence below.

You handwriting is neatly written.

QUESTION 2

Direction: Underline the adverb in the sentence below.

The snow fell, steadily, and December had not even started.

QUESTION 3

Direction: Underline the adverb in the sentence below.

My brother drives very carefully as he has been in car accidents in the past.

Part C – Verbs

QUESTION 1

Direction: Underline the verb in the sentence below.

You handwriting is neatly written.

QUESTION 2

Direction: Underline the verb in the sentence below.

The snow fell steadily, and December had not even started.

QUESTION 3

Define verb.

action

Part D – Pronouns

QUESTION 1

Direction: Change the underline word/words to a pronoun.

Jake played outside with <u>Matt and Blake</u>.

them

QUESTION 2

Direction: Underline the pronoun in the sentence below.

Coming home from camp, he was not happy to his room empty.

QUESTION 3

Direction: Underline the pronoun in the sentence below.

I was not going to work with Jenny for my science project; Jenny is very mean.

keep up good work

Part E – Nouns

QUESTION 1

Direction: Underline the noun in the sentence below.

Last night, the sky was very cloudy, and rain poured all night due to the tropical storm.

QUESTION 2

Direction: Read the following short paragraph and underline all nouns.

Soccer is played throughout the world, and soccer is a fun sport to play. The basic concept to soccer is two teams playing with a round ball on a field. Each team attempts to put the ball in the other team's goal.

QUESTION 3

Define noun.

person place thing

Some sentences have more than few nouns !!!

This page is intentionally left blank.

Task 3: Part D – Assessment Commentary

Question 1 - Analyzing the Focus Learner's Performance

Part A

The following are objectives measured by the daily assessment records:

Lesson 1

The learning goal is for the focus learner to understand, recognize, and use pronouns, nouns, verbs, adjectives, and adverbs when reading and writing.

Lesson 2

The objective is for the students to gain knowledge related to pronouns and to show competencies by completing a worksheet related to pronouns.

Lesson 3

The objective is for the students to gain knowledge related to verbs and to show competencies by completing a worksheet related to verbs.

Lesson 4

The objective is for the students to gain knowledge related to adverbs and to show competencies by completing a worksheet related to adverbs.

Lesson 5

The learning goal is for the focus learner to understand, recognize, and use pronouns, nouns, verbs, adjectives, and adverbs when reading and writing.

Part B

Not applicable

Part C

Not applicable

Part D

The following shows the worksheet grades received by the focus learner, which shows progression toward the learning goal.

Lesson	Number of Incorrect Questions	Score
1	2 out of 10	80%
2	0 out of 10	100%
3	4 out of 10	60%
4	3 out of 10	70%
5	4 out of 22	82%

Part E

From comparing the table in Part D to the baseline data information, the focus learner has shown improvements in all areas. The student is very good at identifying nouns and pronouns as he received 80% on noun worksheet and 100% on pronoun worksheet. In addition, according to the daily assessment record for lesson 1 and 2, the focus learner was involved in paired and group activities. In the worksheet, the focus learner was required to define the terms, and he performed well; he got all those questions correct. For example, in the selected assessment, the focus learner was asked to define verb, adjective, and noun, which he did correctly. During instruction, anchor charts were used to teach these words. Since the focus learner did well with pronoun in baseline assessment, perhaps a greater challenge is needed in this area by having sentences with multiple pronouns for the focus learner to identity. During instruction, planned support of repetition was used to ensure students gained knowledge related to pronouns. The area the focus learner struggled the most was with verbs, where he received a 60% on the worksheet. The student fails to recognize "to be" "is" " are" or "have been" as verbs. The second area the student can improve on is related to adverbs as the student received a 70%. The focus learner also showed strength in identifying adjectives. As seen from the selected assessment, in Part A, the focus learner only got 2 questions incorrect. When it came to identifying adjectives in simple sentences, the student did not get any question incorrect. The student struggled when asked to identify adjectives in multiple sentences or lists as he got Question 8 and 10 in Part A incorrect. Another support provided to the focus learner was including clear direction to each question.

Part F

Anchor charts were used in each lesson to introduce the parts of speech, which positively impacted the student in defining the term correctly on assessments. As seen in selected assessment, the student did get questions related to defining adjective, noun, and verb correctly.

Group activities and paired activities were undertaken in each lesson, which supported the student in doing well in each of the worksheet. According to the daily assessment records, the focus learner was engaged in group and paired activities. The student was able to apply knowledge and receive feedback during in class activity; this supported the learner in doing well on formal assessments.

In each of the lesson, the strategy of repetition was used to get the focus learner exposed to knowledge related to the parts of speech. Using this planned support positively impacted the student. The student was able to practice identifying parts of speech in different ways, which allowed the learner to gain competencies. Aside from lesson 3 verb worksheet, the student's performance in each of the worksheet was acceptable, and this high performance is linked to using the strategy of repetition. In fact, in lesson 5 worksheet for the verb section, the student got all questions correct. The students undertook multiple activities during instruction to ensure acquisition of knowledge related to the parts of speech.

My focus learner has ADHD, so the student can lose focus. As a result, I clearly stated the direction in each question. This supported the student in fully answering the question per directions.

Question 2 – Feedback to Guide Further Learning

Part A

Evidence of feedback was provided on the focus learner's work sample document.

Part B

During instruction, I informed my focus learner to check his work and try again. I also gave multiple opportunities to correct himself. For each assessment, I encouraged the student to double check his work. This error prevention method supported the student in performing well on the learning goal as in the final assessment for question 3 and 7, the student made mistakes but corrected himself. Throughout the learning segment, I provided the focus learner with clear and direct feedback. In addition, my focus learner loses attention due to having ADHD, so I made sure to include positive feedback to keep him engaged. For example, in the selected assessment for analysis, question 4 and 6, I wrote "Excellent Job." Since my focus learner is visual, I made sure to use check marks for correct answers and crosses for incorrect answers. In addition, since my student has auditory processing disorder, I made sure to provide written feedback (correct answers), so the learner can process the feedback. For example, question 8 and 10 in the adjective section, I corrected the student's work. One area the student needs to continue to work on is when there are multiple parts of speech that need to be identified. I directly pointed that out on the student's work sample to ensure the learner sees his mistake.

Part C

During paired activity and group activity, I constantly provided the student with feedback to be able to use in future activities within the lesson and other lessons within the learning segment. To ensure that the feedback was being received and understood, I asked the focus learner if he understood what I stated.

In addition, in each lesson, I included activities where the focus learner was self-grading. In that process, I made sure to provide feedback on student's strength and weakness. In lesson 5 worksheet, the student was able to apply all the feedback provided as I included questions that tested student's knowledge on nouns, pronouns, verbs, adverbs, and adjectives. Based on the table above, the student did not show any major gaps in the assessment completed in lesson 5.

One of the needs of the student is being able to identify multiple parts of speech in sentences, so I included in-class activities to address that. In doing so, I also provided feedback to the student when he was correct or incorrect. In future assignments, I will be including sentences with multiple parts of speech to identify to allow the student to continuously use feedback given.

One of the main feedbacks during instruction was informing the student to double check answers. The student used the feedback in the worksheet completed in lesson 5, and rechecking work will be relevant in future tasks in any subject. In lesson 5, the student erased some of his answers and corrected himself (Question 3 and 7 in Part A). The corrections guide the student towards improving upon his mistakes for subsequent learning.

The overall performance of the student was acceptable. Nothing suggested major gaps in content. Therefore, the best way for the focus learner to apply the feedback is to have subsequent assignments focusing more on lengthy sentences. The sentences used in worksheets were not very lengthy. This will allow the student to apply feedback but also challenge the student.

Question 3 – Evidence of Use of the Expressive/Receptive Communication Skill

Part A

The communication skill required to participate in learning tasks and demonstrate learning was to select the correct parts of speech. The student was shown a poster, and the student was required to select the adverb in the sentence displayed (Task 2 Video Clip 1: timestamp: 3:15). In addition, on the Smart Board, a sentence was displayed for the student to select the adverb (Task 2 Video Clip 1: timestamp: 6:15). The focus learner was involved in paired activity in which he had to select the adverb (Task 2 Video Clip 1: timestamp: 10:00 – 12:00). In lesson 5, the student was involved in paired activity in which he had to select the adjective in sentences (Task 2 Video Clip 2: timestamp: 0:00-4:00). The student was required to use the communication skill of selecting parts of speech in the worksheet assignment for lesson 5 (Student Sample Work). The student was required to underline the parts of speech, which is linked to selecting.

Part B

Anchor charts were used during instruction to support the student in understanding (receptive communication) the key knowledge related to the parts of speech, which supported the student in effectively using communication skill of selecting parts of speech (Task 2 Video Clip 1: timestamp: 0:50). My student is a visual learner and also has auditory processing disorder, so visual aids support his needs.

Paired activities and group activities engage the focus learner to use expressive communication skill to acquire knowledge related to parts of speech, which supported him in using the communication skill of selecting parts of speech in multiple activities (Task 2 Video Clip 1: timestamp: 6:15). In addition, this supported him to perform well on the worksheet assignments (See table above in Question 1 Part D).

In lesson 1 and 3, I had the student read informational text, which required receptive communication skill. The student was required to identify the parts of speech in the text. The student struggles with identifying multiple parts of speech, so this activity supported an area he needed to improve on. In lesson 5 worksheet, the student was required to read short paragraphs prior to selecting the parts of speech (Worksheet Selected Questions 7 and 8 – Part A).

Part C

I also used videos to help the student gain knowledge of selecting parts of speech along with practicing selecting parts of speech. This was a different way of learning, so the student was able to generalize the skill of selecting parts of speech.

The concept of learning via repetition was included in all lessons in the learning segment, which supported the student in maintain communication skill. In each lesson, the student was involved in multiple activities in selecting the parts of speech. For example, in lesson 4, the student was involved in selecting adverb via poster and Smart Board. Then, the student was involved in paired activity requiring selecting parts of speech.

Another way I used repetition was in assessments. In fact, in lesson 5 worksheet, I had sections of students revisiting selecting nouns, pronouns, verbs, and adverbs. This approach supported my student in maintain communication skill (Sample Work Part A).

Having the student identify more than 1 adjective in lesson 5 worksheet engaged the student to apply skill in different setting. This was a way for the student to generalize the skill acquired of selecting adjectives.

Question 4 – Using Assessment to Inform Instruction

The following are next steps to instruction to improve and continue learning:

- The student needs to have direct instruction related to verbs and adverbs as the student's worksheet assignment grade showed weakness in those areas. The student received a 60% on verbs and a 70% on adverbs.

- Since the student is weak in finding multiple parts of speech of same kind, I recommend that the student be engaging in a lesson just targeting looking at paragraphs and finding all the nouns, pronouns, verbs, adverbs, and adjectives. This will engage the student in bettering his skills.

- Differentiation is a key component in learning. Research done by Carol Ann Tomlinson emphasized that differentiation is tailoring instruction to meet individual needs. Differentiation is a way for teacher to respond to students' learning needs. In this case, using a different activity can help the focus learner generalize the knowledge in a different setting. I do think that having the focus learner involved in a different activity besides reading text or index card might benefit him in applying skills acquired in different setting. Perhaps the student can play a jeopardy game with all the parts of speech.

- The student's overall progress was acceptable in the learning segment. However, very few of the sentences were challenging or lengthy. So, I recommend to have the student complete some activities identifying parts of speech with longer sentences. In fact, Piaget's theory of constructivism indicates challenging the students make them effective critical thinkers. Social learning theories are also linked to instructor selecting meaningful and challenging tasks for the students to work on.

Part B

No major implications or changes are required in the student's IEP goals/curriculum. Only documentation is required that states the student has performed acceptable in identifying nouns, pronouns, verbs, adverbs, and adjectives. He can continue to practice these parts of speech, but can move onto more complex form of the parts of speech such as irregular nouns, regular nouns, abstract nouns, regular verbs, and irregular verbs.

This page is intentionally left blank.

Special Education edTPA® Score and Evaluation Analysis

The Special Education edTPA® portfolio received a score of 54. With edTPA® being a subjective exam, the score can be in the range of 52-55 depending on the grader. In all States and university programs, this edTPA® portfolio is considered passing.

Below is a table that breaks down the scores for each rubric. The rubric numbers are referenced only, so candidates are recommended to refer to the handbook for details on the rubrics.

Rubric	Score	Comments/Analysis
1	4	The candidate planned very strong lessons that included various activities to maximize opportunities to develop toward the learning goal. The goal, standard, objectives, planned supports, and learning activities are consistently aligned with each other. All lesson objectives were linked to completing a worksheet, which was measureable. The lesson plans were designed to move the learner toward achieving the learning goal.
2	4	The instructional tasks and supports were used to target the focus learner's learning needs, language needs, interests, and strengths. The candidate took into account focus learner's personal, community, and culture assets to design instruction. The planned supports (videos, anchor charts, paired activities, and group activities) used are connected to the objectives to achieve the learning goal. The supports also were included to challenge the student to better himself. To obtain a 5, the candidate needed to engage the focus learner in self-managing planned supports.
3	4	The candidate took into account focus learner's personal, community, and culture assets along with prior knowledge to design instruction. In the planning commentary, Question 3, the candidate justifies how knowledge of focus learner guided the development of plans. A decent connection to theories was made in the response. In addition, the candidate justifies selection of planned strategies that allow the development of maintained, generalized, and self-directed use of knowledge.
4	4	The candidate mentions the communication skill of selecting parts of speech. A stronger connection is made regarding how the supports address development of communication skill. To obtain a score of 5, the candidate needs to describe in detail how the planned supports are designed to move the focus learner toward maintained or generalized use of the communication skill.
5	4	In each lesson, the candidate used informal and formal assessments. The baseline data and daily assessment records align to the objectives of the lessons. Worksheets are graded to see how the focus learner is progressing toward the learning goal at different points in the learning segment. To obtain a better score,

		the candidate needs to do a better job in reflecting appropriate levels of challenge and supports in light of the focus leaner's strengths, needs, and lesson objectives. The focus learner was involved in monitoring his own progress in a developmentally appropriate way by self-grading.
6	4	Throughout the video, the candidate establishes a positive atmosphere. For example, the candidate discusses good social behaviors. Moreover, the candidate did a good job showing rapport with and respect for all learners. To get a better score, the activities can be more challenging.
7	4	Engagement is shown throughout the video clips. The candidate uses strategies to ensure the focus learner maintains knowledge by using repetition. The candidate explains how the learning is linked to prior learning and personal asset.
8	3	The candidate asks questions and provides feedback to the focus learner, which is seen in the videos. The feedback is not detailed. Not many examples exist in the videos that show the focus learner applying the feedback. The candidate can provide more individualized feedback to obtain a better score for this rubric.
9	4	The candidate did a very good job with learning tasks and instructional strategies to support the learning for the learning goal. Using videos and anchor charts supported focus learners needs. Paired activities and group activities supported his strength areas. The student has autism and auditory processing disorder, and those were taken into account when designing and instructing lessons.
10	4	The candidate included the changes and reasons for the changes. Justification was connected to students' performance and research/theories.
11	3	The candidate provides strong data showing evidence of learning related to the learning goal. In addition, Question 1 Part D, the candidate provided data showing progressing toward the learning goal. In addition, the candidate references baseline data to compare data. The analysis fails to discuss levels or types of supports to understand the focus leaner's progressing toward all objectives.
12	3	When giving feedback, the candidate was focused more on just looking for mistakes and correcting the mistakes. To obtain a better score, the candidate needs to provide feedback that connects to strengths and needs of the focus student.
13	3	Feedback was provided to the focus learner, and opportunities existed to allow the focus learner to use feedback. However, the candidate did not focus on having the student apply feedback on their strengths or weaknesses.
14	3	The candidate does a good job in getting the focus student to use communication skill along with planned supports. Evidence was provided in multiple forms to show use of communication skill and planned supports.
15	3	The next steps of instruction were general along with the research/theories. To

		obtain better score, the candidate needs to provide a stronger connection to research/theories.
Total Score	56	This edTPA® is a strong portfolio with a score of 54. The lesson plans were very well developed to ensure the focus learner was developing related to the learning goal. Learning tasks, supports, strategies, and assessments were used that targeted the focus student's learning needs and language needs. Video clips were provided showing the candidate providing a positive and safe learning environment that engaged the focus student in objectives related to the learning goal. Throughout the learning segment, the candidate conducted assessments to ensure focus student's learning. The commentary responses were well written with details.

This page is intentionally left blank.

Chapter 14 - Special Education Lesson Plan Template

Lesson Title

Grade Level

Learning Goal

Objective

Educational Standard

Instructional Materials/Resources

Instructional Procedures (detail steps to instruction)

Instructional Strategies (what instructional strategies will be used in the lesson)

Communication Skill and Planned Supports

Generalization, Maintenance, and/or Self-Directed Use of Knowledge and Skills

Assessments (Formal and Informal)

9 781087 817224